Endorsements

I have cherished my friendship with Susy over these many years. Through thick and thin, I've watched her pour her life and heart into God and the people around her. Countless times, she has ministered to me out of His love that flows through her. Susy is a living testimony of "Yea, though I walk through the valley of the shadow of death, I will fear no evil, for You are with me." I've watched her overcome heartache and hardship time and time again, leaning into God for strength and comfort, and then turning right around and pouring it out on others in the midst of her own trials. Susy's story grabs your heart, causing you to not want to stop reading until you have finished the book! She is an amazing woman of God who has weathered the dark night of the soul and come out shining in God"s love and light! Susy is truly a living example of God's grace and love, which is available to us all…if we but ask.

JoAnn McFatter

God said that He hates divorce. However, divorce has been the new normal, even in Christian marriages, when reconciliation fails. But God never fails. Susy shares her journey of learning to walk with Jesus by faith, even through the trials of a divorce.

Oon Theam Khoo,
Spiritual Father to Susy

Susy's life story will inspire, entertain, and encourage you. She is an overcomer, living life with great passion. Susy has opened her heart to the readers, becoming very vulnerable by sharing her journey with all its ups and downs. I've had the privilege of walking with her on part of this journey, and I know Susy to be both funny and tenacious. Let her humor, and her example of perseverance, bring the same healing to your soul that it has to her own. Laughter truly is the best medicine! I know this isn't the end of the story, and I look forward to walking with her into the sequel.

Kari Browning, Director
New Renaissance Healing & Creativity Center
Coeur d'Alene, Idaho

Susy has been a good friend of mine for thirteen years. We've walked through the storms of life together, which not only deepened our friendship but our faith in Jesus. Susy is my "Energizer Bunny", because she keeps on going no matter what obstacles get in her way. From the broken pieces of her life, God has created a beautiful mosaic. The valleys have drawn Susy very close to her Shepherd, grazing in His green pastures and resting in His loving arms. Jesus has restored the "joy of her salvation" and redeemed the years the locusts have eaten.

Susy is the most generous person I've ever known, and I believe this is just the beginning of the Lord's favor. Praise the Lord! I love you Susy!

Joy Proeschel

In this book, you will read about a beautiful woman who is multi-talented, powerful, tenderhearted, giving, resourceful, loving, gifted, a tremendous mom, and loves Jesus with all of her heart. You will read her love story as it began, unfolds, and then falls apart. You will get to know Susy. Her story is one that will captivate you through the final page.

I've known Susy for a long time. I've seen her pain, as her marriage did indeed fall apart, resulting in divorce. Now I see a woman who is back, healed, and more beautiful than ever, who is looking forward to a full new life as a mom and fulfilled wife. As you get to know Susy, you will love her as I do. Go for it, girl!

Jeanne Schletty

I found myself captivated by Susy's true life, fairytale love story that began at such a young age. Her unique style of writing will draw you into her story, as if you are reliving each moment with her. Every girl dreams of finding the man who will sweep her off of her feet and marry her. Then they are supposed to live happily ever after...but many times people change and divorce happens. Since 2006, I have had the privilege of working with Susy professionally in real estate and as a volunteer in conference ministry. I have witnessed firsthand many of the ups and downs as they happened in Susy's life. Her journey through divorce has changed her in many ways... for the better. She is a happier, stronger, and more self-confident woman and I am so proud of her accomplishments. There is nothing fake about Susy; she is very real and truly loves the Lord with all of her heart. Her life story gives hope and inspiration to anyone going through a life-changing event. I have never met anyone like Susy and I am so thankful to be able to call her my close friend.

Rhonda Anderson

Out *of the* Cookie, Into *the* Fortune

FINDING YOUR TREASURE WITHIN

From the Heart of

Susy Pujiro

Out of the Cookie, Into the Fortune

Email: susysblog@gmail.com
Follow her Blog: susysthinkingplace.com
Twitter: @susypujiro

Cover image: BigStock #14882729
Cover and book design by Jeff Doles
www.ChristianBookDesign.com

Contents

Foreword

Much like Susy Pujiro, who never intended to write this book, I (of all people) never banked on writing the Foreword. As far as I was concerned, there is a plethora of people much more suited for the job than I. The last thing I ever intended was to add my name to the long list of those who had undertaken such endeavors.

THEN, EVERYTHING CHANGED...
I MET SUSY AND HER HUSBAND.

Love is a decision, a commitment. The feeling of being in love is a byproduct of acting upon that commitment, that decision. Sadly, when one spouse allows a break in character and consciously walks away from their commitment, dreams get destroyed, families get hurt, and worlds get turned upside down.

Suddenly, issues that a person had wrestled with in the course of their life, and questions that may have long since been put to rest, rise up again and overflow in the ending of a marriage. The constant changes, suffering and loss can be like repetitively tearing the bandages off of old wounds, adding to the hurt and injury that were already there. And, often this produces a lost sense of direction; an inability to find a level horizon or to get one's compass pointing true north again. Crash landed, bruised and torn, the wounded stumbles wondering if they'll ever get back in the air again, questioning God's plan.

IT'S NOT JUST THE BLIND MAN WHO LOSES HIS SIGHT.

For Susy, the journey that was ahead became a realization the first time she spoke the word "divorce" out loud. The world she and her husband had built was now failed...and she so desperately wanted that not to be true. Yet, her brightest dreams and greatest fears stood just around the corner. And, without a strong conviction of heart, she might have found herself standing mute, driven by hopes, and silenced by doubts.

On the surface, Susy's story may not seem unique. Being on the receiving end of a dissolved marriage is almost commonplace today. But that is just on the surface; her story goes much deeper than that. Hers is a story of personal legacy, a legacy of understanding and truly appreciating the power of love. Of extending grace and kindness...of character developed in the crucible. In Romans 5, God has great words for those who are suffering, "But we also exalt in our tribulations, knowing that tribulation brings about perseverance; and perseverance, proven character; and proven character, hope." We find a hint of God's plan in Romans. He certainly has His reasons for hardship, misunderstanding, loss, and pain. And, there are times when those things just simply cause us to take the baton.

Susy's story isn't as much about her passing tests and preserving trials, as it is with her passing the baton. Her story "cuts a trail" around the track for us to see the direction to go, and with that, our responsibility to take the baton and run...to wisely recognize and use the fortunes that God provides.

One thing you will learn from Susy is that what we want to do isn't nearly as important as what we want to become. It's possible to do a lot of things in life, yet to be zero as a person. Doing is tied closely with activity, accomplishments, and tangible things; such as salary, prestige, trophies and records. Being, on the other hand, has more to do with intangibles; the kind of people we become down inside...much of which cannot be measured by objective tallies, wealth, and impressive awards. Of the two, being will ultimately out distance doing every time. This is her fortune, her legacy. For if we learn anything from Susy, we learn that isolation is not how to live your life emotionally, physically, or with God.

Susy is not an isolationist. Her story is a refusal to keep to herself. She knows that the key to life is through the sharing of oneself. This, by the way, is exactly what living is really all about. In spite of her trials, Susy builds bridges wherever she goes. And through the pages of her story, we now have the baton.

As you read, please remember that God's heart is especially tender toward the downtrodden and the defeated. He has seen and felt every tear shed. He is there when things take a wrong turn. God speaks directly to us out of the mouth of the prophet Jeremiah (29:11), "For I know the plans I have for you," declares the Lord, "plans to prosper you and not to harm you, plans to give you hope and a future." I encourage you to take acknowledgement of a life being fully lived and a call to action ~ to extend and multiply the legacy that Susy has set forth for all of us. For that, my friends, is the true fortune.

Thomas A. Colbert
Burnsville, Minnesota

Acknowledgements

"SOME PEOPLE COME INTO OUR LIVES AND QUICKLY GO. SOME STAY FOR A WHILE AND LEAVE FOOTPRINTS ON OUR HEARTS. AND WE ARE NEVER, EVER THE SAME." ~ *Anonymous*

Words cannot express my gratitude to each one of you who have touched my heart and made my life rich. You left your footprints on my heart, and my life will never be the same. I am forever grateful to all of you who have played an integral part in my life:

Michael, Daniel, David, and Kyle, my children ~ You have enriched my life, and I wouldn't trade being your mother for anything else in this world. I'm so blessed to have all of you in my life. I love you.

Mary Pujiro, my mother ~ Thank you for your love and words of wisdom. I wouldn't be who I am today without you. You taught me generosity and how to love. I wish I could hear you say, "Everything will be okay" one more time. I miss you so much!

Basirun Pujiro, my father ~ Thank you for your love and support. You foresaw my future when you decided to send me to an English class. You taught me how to be independent and courageous. I love you!

Papa Khoo Oon Theam, my spiritual father ~ Thank you for being a father to me, which is a role that you don't take lightly. Your words of encouragement and prayers are greatly appreciated. Thank you for believing in me.

Nontje Tunas ~ You are a sweetheart! Thank you so much for being there for me and my children. Without you, I wouldn't be able to soar as high as I can with God. Your prayers are much appreciated. I love you.

Tom Colbert ~ Thank you for taking the time to just listen when I babbled. Your encouragement, advice, and our long talks about life were priceless. Without you, this book wouldn't have been written or published.

Jeanne Schletty ~ Thank you for being there in my darkest hours. Your prayers and your presence were the calm in the storm. I will never forget the time when I was crying, and I told you that I missed my mother. You quickly replied, "If that's what you need, I'll be your mother."

Joy Proeschel ~ I thank God for letting our paths cross. You have been more than a best friend to me; you are my big sister. You were there through all my darkest hours. I knew that I could always call you, no matter what time it was. Your words calmed my soul.

Rhonda Anderson ~ Thank you for your sound advice and for being there for me. You always call and make it a point to see me whenever you are in town for our girl's time and long talks. I treasure our time together.

Mieke and Andi Kangwijaya ~ Thank you both for all your help and support during my divorce. Mieke, you're like the little sister I never had. You are sweet and always eager to help me with anything that you can. Thank you for listening to me and for lending me your shoulder to cry on. We've had fun times together and I miss you a lot.

Rinto and Nike Dasuki ~ Thank you for showing me what unconditional love is; your actions speak louder than your words. I treasure our friendship.

Kari Browning ~ You are a gem! The day that you heard I was going through a divorce, you flew in to comfort me. I will never forget that. You are a true friend and I'm blessed to have met you.

JoAnn McFatter ~ Out of sight, but not out of mind…even though you travel a lot, you always took the time to check in and see how I was doing. You were always asking what you could do for me. Thank you for praying for me and for being there when I needed you.

Vincetta Christopherson ~ My worst critique, but I love how your insight and thinking challenge me. You are always taking pictures and catching the moments perfectly. You are part of our family.

Cris Marlette ~ My very first friend in America. Thank you for your kindness and love. You made it easier to live in America. I miss our coffee and cookie chats.

Noy Gilmore ~ Thank you for your generosity and kindness. You taught me a lot about cooking and treated me like family.

To my friends Jan, Cecilia, Lynn and many others: Thank you for your kind words and for being there for me. But most importantly, thank you for believing in me. May each of you find the path leading to your destiny and learn to soar like eagles.

Carole Robbins ~ My editor and newly-found friend. Words can't express how much I appreciate your dedication to helping me with this book. We had a good time collaborating, and I know this isn't the only book that we will be working on together. Thank you from the bottom of my heart.

Note: Some of the names in this book have been changed to conceal personal identities.

Introduction

L ife is full of surprises with its twists and turns, highs and lows, and mountains and valleys. Sometimes, in the midst of an ordinary life, a curveball is thrown your way that takes your breath away and knocks you off your feet. The outcome of your life will be determined by how you respond to that curveball.

I am the mother of four beautiful children ages 21, 19, 17, and 13 years old. However, life wouldn't be complete without pets; we have four dogs of different sizes that we love very much. I was married for twenty-two years, and I always thought that my marriage would last until "death do us part". Never in a million years did I imagine that I would get divorced. Our marriage wasn't perfect, but we were a happy family most of the time. We built our real estate business together, and we worked as a team for twenty-two years. We thought that by working together, we were also building our relationship. That concept was wrong, because we never really had the chance to get to know each other. We needed to nurture our relationship, in order to know and understand each other. Relationships aren't built running on autopilot.

As I looked back on our marriage, I can see that it was much more about building a business than building a lasting relationship. I thought we had it all, until my world was shaken. Seven months after it ended, I found out my husband was having an affair with a younger woman. Why didn't I see any clues or suspicious behavior? I can only say that I truly loved and trusted my husband with all my heart. He was the love of my life…Boy, was I ever wrong!

"LOVE AND TRUST CAN BLIND YOUR JUDGMENT"

In my life experience, it was the lessons I learned from the curveball that built me up as a person. As I found out what I was made of, I found myself again. The lessons weren't easy, but now that it's over, I can clearly see the blue sky again and the horizon is full of promises.

"THROUGH TRIALS AND TRIBULATIONS, YOU FIND WHO YOU ARE AGAIN"

Would any of us want to go through it, if we knew the trials and challenges we would face in life? It might be too difficult to think about, or even imagine, how we could come out whole. I have learned that it's possible to go through the mountains and valleys of life, and the curveballs can become blessings in disguise.

During one of my counseling sessions, the title of this book was born. When I mentioned to my counselor that I should probably write a book because my life had become so interesting, he thought for a few seconds and said, "Why don't you?" I asked, "If I were to write a book, what would the title be?" My counselor said he didn't know, but a few seconds later he said, "Out of the Cookie, Into the Fortune". Thus, the title of this book was born on November 11, 2011 at 10:11 AM.

I wasn't in a hurry to write this book, as the holidays were coming up. My plan was to write the book after the holidays. It just so happened that I was talking with a friend of mine who had recently published her book. She suggested that I call her editor, so I did. I wanted to hire the editor to be my ghost writer, but he immediately said no and asked me what I knew about writing a book. I told him that I knew nothing, so he suggested that I go to his class about writing books. I gladly went to his class and it was very beneficial for me.

I still wasn't rushing into writing a book, as I just didn't want to write a book for the sake of writing. I wanted my book to have substance that would inspire and encourage people. So I told God that I just couldn't write a book without substance, and He had to tell me what my fortune was. A few months went by, and one day He told me that my fortune was finding myself again. I looked back at my life and where I am today, and I pondered how I had indeed found myself again.

You see, I thought that I would be writing a book four to five years down the road when I had already established myself. However, God's thoughts and ways of doing things are much different than mine. Since 2008, God had tricked me into writing a journal, and then I started to write comments on someone's blog. After a while, I realized I had followers. They enjoyed reading what I had to say, so it seemed natural for me to convey my thoughts and feelings about different subjects.

"GOD'S THOUGHTS AND WAYS ARE HIGHER THAN OUR THOUGHTS AND WAYS"

My hope is that you will find little nuggets in this book that will encourage and inspire you to not only find your destiny, but the fortune that is hidden in your heart. My prayer is that you will fulfill your dreams and destiny, becoming who you truly are on the inside; one who is fearfully and wonderfully made by God. Also, remember to smile…it's free and it brightens everyone's day!

Chapter 1

I Can Finally Breathe

April 3, 2012 ~ The weather was cloudy and cold, but I had given Bruno permission to come and shampoo the carpet anyhow. I was dragging because I had gone to bed at 2:30 AM. There was just so much to be done, as I raced against time to meet the deadlines imposed by the attorneys. There were copies to be made, neglected bills were going unpaid, and there was paperwork everywhere that needed to be put away again. The paperwork itself was overwhelming, not to mention the emotional roller coaster, as you speed blindly through the dark tunnel of divorce. How would I survive this emotional turmoil with sanity, when was it going to end, and was it possible to ever be happy again?

"THERE IS LIGHT AT THE END OF THE TUNNEL"

My husband Jake had a hard time signing the divorce papers.

If he didn't go through with the signing today, I had no choice but to take him to court. A motion would then be brought before the judge ordering him to sign the papers; the court date was scheduled for April 5, 2012.

So, here I am waiting for the phone call from my attorney to let me know if Jake had signed the divorce papers. It's a bittersweet day, as the nightmare was ending, and I'm free to pursue my dreams and destiny, but it's also sad at the same time. It was the end of twenty-two years of marriage to the love of my life…the man who stole my heart the first time I saw him at the airport in Indonesia. It's not easy to just wipe out 22 years of life together, which included four wonderful children and mountains of memories…some good, some bad, and some ugly.

I signed my divorce papers yesterday and the feeling was so deliberating that I know I'm now on the path to my destiny. Am I scared? Yes, but I know that God is with me; He has been there for me through this entire process and He will help me through this as well.

"EVEN THOUGH YOU CAN'T FEEL HIM, GOD HAS BEEN THERE FOR YOU ALL ALONG"

I am so thankful that I have God in my life! Without Him, I would have been admitted to a mental institution or would have required drugs to calm my anxiety. He has been the best medicine for me, as I have learned to put my trust in Him and lean upon Him daily. God also provided a very loving network of friends to support me; they gave me shoulders to cry on, gentle pats on the back to say it would all be okay, and food for my body and soul. They have always been there in my times of need.

"GOOD FRIENDS ARE THERE THROUGH THICK AND THIN AND THEY DON'T COUNT THE COST"

It has been a very long, hard journey, and I wouldn't wish the treacherous path I've been down on anyone. I have felt the world crumbling under my feet and I didn't know how I could possibly survive. Questions flooded my mind and I wondered what I had done wrong in my marriage. Could I have turned back the hands of time and made everything all right? If I had just held on a little longer, if I had been more patient and let him work things out in his heart, would he have come back so we could be a family again?

As a dark storm is passing, a rainbow of promise fills the sky, as the sun shines through the last lingering tears of rain. Divorce works the same way, but the promise is that you are free from the agony of a bad relationship, whether it's physical abuse, emotional abuse or adultery. You have been set free from the emotional roller coaster and there's a brighter future awaiting you. Sailing through life won't be easy now that you are alone with your children. How are you going to survive? How are we going to make it alone? Fear and doubt now haunt you about your decision to sign the papers; was it the right or wrong thing to do? "What if's" continually flood your mind, but you have to trust your decision and not succumb to doubt.

It takes courage to walk away from any relationship, whether it's a good or bad one. We tend to want to ride it out, hoping the other person will change and that everything will be okay and get better. Sometimes things work out, but sometimes you can't avoid the inevitable divorce. In my case, the divorce couldn't be avoided, even though I was hoping that Jake would change his mind and things would work out. We tend to paint a picture of what our lives should be, but the detours and bumps in the road alter our plans. I have learned that plans don't change, but people do, and you have no control over another person's feelings.

"AFTER THE STORM, THE RAINBOW COMES WITH A PROMISE"

As the memories of what had transpired the last five years of our marriage flooded my mind, I was able to look at each memory, whether good or bad, and smile or cry at the same time. I realized that there were more good memories than bad, but God's grace had erased the painful sting of the bad ones. When I look at the bad times, I can smile and say it was hard, yet something good has come out of it. Those memories are pieces of my life's tapestry.

"MEMORIES ARE PIECES OF LIFE'S TAPESTRY"

As I go through my day now, I notice there is no longer any anxiety and I'm as calm as I can be. The inner peace, which only God can impart, has been the strong tower that protected me, and I know that I'm at peace with the divorce. As a free woman, I'm ready to embark upon an exciting new journey. I'm ready to fulfill the purpose for my life that has been predestined before the foundation of the earth. I realize that freedom isn't cheap…it costs you everything, but it's worth it all.

"INNER PEACE COMES FROM TRUSTING GOD"

Just as a captive bird flees its cage and stands on the treetops viewing the vast horizon for the first time, I realized that I'm free and I can fly anywhere I want to! As a free woman with dreams and a destiny, there is a new world out there just waiting to be discovered and explored! Ever since I stepped foot in America to marry Jake, I realized that I was never given the choice to pursue my passions and giftings. Instead, those hopes and desires had been put aside, and I was quite content being Jake's wife and assistant, raising a family and helping him fulfill his aspirations. I thought my marriage would be "until death do us part"...Boy, was I wrong! People change, situations change, and new challenges arise that can alter your dreams and consequently the outcome of your life.

"THINGS DON'T CHANGE BUT PEOPLE DO, AND YOU HAVE NO CONTROL OVER IT"

Now I am alone and free...free to decide what I want to do with my life. Who am I now? I lost my identity as a woman and as a person, and I need to redefine my purpose and calling. When you have lived in the shadow of your spouse for so long, it's hard to come out of that shadow and stand alone. I thought the world of Jake, but as I looked back, I can see how naïve I was about his behavior and the way he treated me. I was just too caught up in the tumultuousness of life; growing a business, raising my children, running a house, and just caring for everyone...including the pets. I always believed that Jake loved me with his whole heart, and most importantly, I trusted him with my life.

"WHEN YOU LOVE SOMEONE, YOU TRUST THEM BLINDLY"

After having gone through all of this, I learned that we should always retain our own identity, and as a married couple, we have joint dreams, destiny and identity. Now that I am on a journey to find myself again, I'm excited about what life will bring into this new chapter of my life. Sometimes when a door closes, a new door opens with better opportunities. We tend to become comfortable in one spot, or stuck in a rut, and we don't really want to move or change. When your world is suddenly shaken and falling apart, you have no choice but to go with it and find new ground. For me, that new ground was to find myself again and live my life to its fullest, as if it's the only day I have.

"WHEN YOUR WORLD IS SHAKEN AND FALLING APART, FIND NEW GROUND"

Life is a gift from above, so we can enjoy God's creation. Because each day is a unique gift, I don't complain, no matter how bad my day has been. I've learned that since the beginning of time, we were only given two choices…good or evil, black or white, and happy or sad. The choices are simple, but we tend to make them too complicated. No matter how terrible my day has been, even if I have just had the biggest fight ever with Jake, I always said to myself "Today is another day and I can get through today". Another gift that God has given me is the ability to sleep. No matter how hard the situation is or how awful the day has been, when I lay my head on the pillow, I can sleep and become refreshed. God knows what I need and He provides for me.

"LIFE IS PRECIOUS AND A GIFT FROM GOD"

As I sit on the sofa of my porch overlooking the lake, the water is very calming and tranquil. I reflect on memories of our lives together; the family God gave us, the successful business we created, and the shaking of our marriage. All in all, my life has been good. As memories of our marriage flood my mind, I drift through the tunnel of time, as I contemplate my life's journey.

"LIFE IS FULL OF SURPRISES, EMBRACE IT WITH A SMILE"

Chapter 2

Life is Simple and Ordinary

Life in Indonesia was quite simple; we were far from being rich and yet we weren't poor either. I lived in a small house full of love with four older sisters and two brothers. As you have probably already guessed, I was the youngest girl in the family. We learned to share and prioritize the shower in the morning, based upon the first to go to work or elsewhere. Some of my siblings slept in bunk beds, with my older brother on the top bunk, while I shared a queen-sized bed with my two older sisters. We were very close growing up, and we liked to snuggle with each other and tell stories. Family time was always spent telling stories about events of the day or reminiscing about relatives. My mother would tell stories about how my grandpa and grandma were merchants from China and how they opened a grocery store in Indonesia.

"THE BEST MEMORIES ARE THE SIMPLE THINGS THAT BRING SMILES AND WARM THE HEART"

My mother stayed at home with us, she was very good at managing money, and we always had what we needed. It might not be fancy, but we always had food to eat and never went hungry. Before she married my father, my mother used to own a dry cleaning business. She had endured a lot in her life, but she was a strong woman of integrity, and a good mother to all of us. My mother taught us lessons about life, and she instilled the wisdom and core values that I've carried through my adult life and imparted into my own children.

"YOU ARE RICH, WHEN YOU HAVE LOVE AND FAMILY"

When I was growing up, I remember my mother saving her money and forgetting about it until she really needed it. Then she would take the money out of her jar and buy food or pay bills with it. Whenever she had some extra money, my mother would take me shopping and buy me five to six dresses for me to go to my English lessons. She told me that if I had six outfits, then I could alternate wearing them, and I would be the best dressed girl in the class.

"A MOTHER'S LOVE TRANSCENDS TO ETERNITY"

I didn't know much about my father's background, other than he was born on the Island of Sumatra. He only had a 5th grade education, but he owned a construction company and was very successful. He had his own driver to take him around from one job site to another, and he ran a crew of 200 people. My father did all the bidding, and his workmanship had an excellent reputation. While he was working on a street project by her business, my father fell in love with my mother.

My father had two wives…he had three children with his first wife, and yes, my mother was his other wife. I never saw my life as any different from the lives of my friends, except that my father didn't sleep in our home, which was always a full house. Can you imagine eight of us in a small house with two bedrooms and one bath? I grew up being loved by my mother and my siblings. I had an abundance of older siblings to play with me and love me, so I never felt deprived of love.

Our house had an open kitchen, or the equivalent of a deck in America, which meant that the ceiling was the sky. The roof of our house was tiled, but sometimes those tiles broke. Consequently, when it rained, we had to use buckets to catch the water coming into the house. There wasn't much to do when it rained, except snuggle in our beds and tell stories. My mother would buy corn and boil it. We would listen to her stories while we ate the corn. When it rained, we also had to use an umbrella to go to the bathroom… imagine that! Even though the house was very modest, love and laughter were there. I think those were the best times of my life growing up. Life was simple and full of love.

Another fond memory from my childhood was playing in the rain. Summer in Indonesia was quite hot, so when we got rain in the summer, my friends and I would run around the houses playing in it. We would stand under the gutters and just let the rainwater pour down on us. It was so much fun! We played in the rain for about 10 - 15 minutes, and then we all went home and took showers. When I crawled in bed, I would listen to the sound of the rain until I fell asleep. There was something about the raindrops hitting the tiled roof that made the most beautiful melody! Now that I'm grown up, I still enjoy listening to the sound of rain hitting the roof, as I'm falling asleep. There is nothing more beautiful than the sound of rain!

"HOME IS WHERE FAMILY GATHERS AND LOVE IS SPOKEN"

I began questioning my mother about my father when I was in fourth grade. In a simple way that I could understand, she explained it to me and I never questioned her again. I guess I had learned to trust at an early age, as I knew I was okay, loved and taken care of. Even though my father didn't sleep in our home, I could see the love between my parents.

As she cooked dinner for him, I would watch my father give my mother kisses and hold her. You see, I learned about love at young age. My parents might not have been the best example of what a marriage should be, but the love they had for each other was enough to give me an ideal picture of what marriage was supposed to be.

"WE ARE MOLDED TO WHAT WE SEE OUR PARENTS DO AND SAY"

As I grew up, I learned that I was born out of wedlock. I didn't know any differently, because I was always loved and cared for by my mother and siblings. As I looked back, I realized that no matter how we came into this world or where we came from, we were not a mistake. I believe every child is born with a destiny. God knew us before we were even formed in our mother's womb, and we were predestined to be born at a specific time in history for God's glory. We all make up a small part of the puzzle in the big picture of life. Our life circumstances may be very different from what we were predestined for, yet the destiny bestowed upon us is always there for us to fulfill.

"YOU ARE NOT A MISTAKE; YOU ARE BORN WITH A PURPOSE"

So, I can rightly say that you are not a mistake, because God has a plan and purpose for your life that only you can fulfill. Don't get discouraged because you aren't like others or your life is hard; God loves you and He smiled the day you were born! Although things in life can alter your dreams, when you make the decision to walk in your destiny, God is with you and He will direct your path. His plan is to prosper and bless you, and His ways are so much higher than we can think or imagine.

"GOD SMILED THE DAY YOU WERE BORN"

The Chinese name that I was born with was Fu Tjuen Siang, which means "Fragrant Summer", and that's the name that my friends at school knew me by. According to my mother, my grandma, who died when I was a year old, loved me very much. Whenever she came to visit, I cried when she wanted to hold me, so she would rub my back, calling me "Sayang" or "love" in Indonesian.

From the soothing words spoken by my grandmother, my nickname "Yayang" was derived, and that is what my family and neighbors called me. It's amazing how this nickname, which also means "love", had to suffer so much for love. But this name actually defines who I am...I've experienced many facets of love. Then I was given an English name, so I guess I've had a name for every season of my life.

When I was in the fourth grade, my father sent me to private lessons to learn the English language. He told me that I would need it to find a good job in the future. A week before the class started,

Yulan, my oldest sister, decided that I needed an English name to go along with my studies. She thought for a while and then announced that my new name should be "Susy", which means Lily. Yulan was very pleased with her choice, so "Susy" became the English name that I'm known by today.

My English Teacher was a very nice woman who took her time teaching me English. So that I could catch up with the other kids in class, she would ask me to come for additional lessons on Saturday morning. I have to admit, I didn't grasp English very well, and I wasn't picking up the lessons as quickly as the other kids. Her patience and love for me though, caused me want to learn and excel in English, which I did.

As for my education, I didn't go to college, but I did finish high school. I chose to go to a vocational high school, instead of regular high school, and I took additional classes in administration and accounting. After I graduated from high school, I started to work for a local company as a typist/secretary; then I got a better job and worked as an executive secretary for a French company. Before I left for America in 1987, I was the personal assistant to a prominent person in Indonesia.

"YOU CAN'T CHOOSE WHAT LIFE GIVES YOU, BUT YOU CAN CHOOSE HOW YOU LIVE WITH IT"

Chapter 3

Love at First Sight

It was Wednesday morning, we had just finished our study group, and we were waiting until it was time to go to school. As we were waiting, one of my friends looked at the newspaper and found an ad that said "Hey ladies, want to correspond with American men? Please send your picture and bio to..." We thought it might be pretty cool to have pen pals in America, plus we would get free stamps.

Some of my friends had pen pals they enjoyed writing to, plus it was a time when collecting foreign stamps was the "in" thing at school. We either bought used stamps with our allowances, or we got free stamps from letters sent by friends or relatives living abroad. It sounded like a good idea to have a pen pal and receive free stamps.

I decided to respond to the ad in the newspaper, and I submitted my picture and bio data to the pen pal club address. A couple months later, I got a letter from the club informing me that they couldn't publish my bio data because I was only 15 years old. Their minimum age requirement was 16 years old, but they said they would keep my profile and publish it the following year. I didn't think they were interested in publishing me, so it became a forgotten subject.

Time went on and a year had gone by. When I came home from school one day, my mom told me that I had gotten a letter from America. I was puzzled because I didn't know anyone in America. She handed me the letter and I opened it. It was a half-page letter from Tom who was 24 years old...he was rather handsome.

It was the start of many letters that I would receive from American men ages 24 - 65 years old. I was thrilled, but collecting stamps had become obsolete by this time, and I no longer had any use for the stamps. I also found it rather strange that I was getting all these letters from older men who wanted to marry me and not a single letter from kids my age.

You see, I had forgotten all about the picture and bio data that I had submitted a year ago. Two weeks later, I received a letter from the pen pal club, along with a brochure showing my picture and bio...they had published me.

My mother offered to pay for the stamps to reply to the letters, as an exercise for my English lessons. I was the only one who took private lessons; no one else in my family spoke English. So even though it was in the form of writing, my mother thought it would be nice for me to practice my English. I felt obligated to write back, so in order to be polite, I began replying to each letter. I guess I was so naïve at 16 years old that I had no idea what I was getting myself into.

After I married Jake, we were talking to some of his friends about how we met. I realized that I was a mail order bride, but he argued that he didn't think so. It was through this pen pal club that I met and found the love of my life, so it was all worth it.

"LOVE COMES IN MANY WAYS, SHAPES AND SIZES"

It was quite an experience for me to write back to these men. I received many kinds of letters (no profane ones) that were nice, but I was more interested in what they were writing to me. Some of the letters were a quarter of a page, some were half a page, and rarely were any of them three quarters of a page long.

This went on for about a year, and then I decided that none of these men interested me; I was 17 years old and they were older than me. It had cost me my allowance and my mom's money for stamps too, so I decided to quit writing to everyone, except a few men who were nice and interesting as pen pals. I wrote to James, who visited me twice in Indonesia; Doug, who was a professor and a very nice man; and Jeff, who was in jail…go figure.

Even though I still received letters, I decided not to write to anyone anymore, and that's when I received a letter from Jake. I found his letter quite interesting and unlike any of the others, plus it was two pages long and typed. Jake also sent a picture of himself wearing a brown suit, holding a briefcase and standing by his car; he was wearing glasses and he was kind of short. If I were to marry an American, my ideal would be someone tall, with blue eyes and blond hair, so I wasn't interested in him.

Jake's letter was interesting, because he wrote about what he hoped to accomplish in his life. He wrote that he wanted to retire at the age of 40, he wanted four children, but he didn't want any nanny taking care of his children, he wanted to travel the world, etc. I read his letter, put it on my study desk and decided not to write him back. After a few days, I threw his letter in the trash can in my room, but then I pulled it out again. For about a month, I would pick it up, read it and put it on my desk again.

"LOVE IS A SPLENDID THING"

Jake was so different from the other men who had written to me. He was able to tell me about the dreams and goals in his life, while the others didn't tell me anything other than they wanted to marry me. My curiosity got the best of me, so I decided to write Jake back and that was the start of our relationship. Jake was a good writer and very persistent. We wrote back and forth for almost a year. He was quick to reply to my letters, and it seemed like before my letter even reached him, I had gotten another letter. This was before the Internet or email existed, so we communicated via snail mail, which took 10 - 14 days for a letter to reach its destination. Jake wrote to me almost every day.

I remember getting letters from him on "Perkins" napkins that were very short just to say "Thinking of you or I miss you". Jake captured my heart with his letters and quick notes. I began to imagine how my life would be with him, because I had started to like him. He sent more pictures of himself and, quite honestly, he wasn't a bad looking guy. I fell in love with him, and I looked forward to coming home from school, because I knew I would get a letter from him. When I didn't get his letters, I would miss him dearly.

"P.S. I LOVE YOU"

Jake was honest with me about an on and off again girlfriend he had who was Japanese. He sent me a picture of him, his sister and his girlfriend. Even though I liked him, I never thought he was serious about me; I thought we were just pen pals.

A few months after we started writing to each other, Jake got saved, his life turned around, and he was on fire for God. He wrote

Christian tracts and a newsletter, which he funded himself, and he was doing street evangelism. I was happy about the change in his life.

"WHEN GOD GETS HOLD OF YOU, LIFE CHANGES"

Jake later told me that he had broken up with his girlfriend. He also said that he loved me and he started talking to me about marriage. For me, it was a little farfetched to be married to someone from America and living there, so I didn't think that would happen. I didn't take Jake seriously, because I realized that he was also writing to a lot of other Asian girls, and he probably said the same things to them.

Because it was very expensive, it was becoming a burden for me to buy stamps. I told Jake that I needed to stop writing to him because I was going to marry James. To tell the truth, I wasn't planning on marrying anyone, because I was still in high school. Jake told me to wait for him, because he was coming to Indonesia to visit me. He said I shouldn't be in a hurry to marry James until I had met him first. I thought this guy was crazy. Well, he was crazy enough to drive from Minnesota to San Francisco nonstop to catch a flight to Indonesia.

In August 1981, Jake showed up at the airport in Indonesia with long hair and glasses. When I saw him for the first time that evening at the airport, I knew right away in my heart that he was the one I would marry and spend the rest of my life with.

"LOVE AT FIRST SIGHT"

Jake stayed with us in our modest home for a month. During that time, he underwent a bit of culture shock. Our bathroom wasn't like the typical bathroom in America. In order to take a shower, we had a tub filled with water, from which we would take a scoop. While we did have running water, it took awhile to refill the tub, so we had to be careful with our water usage. To keep down the algae growth in the tub, it was quite common to put in a couple goldfish.

When it came time for Jake to take a shower, he thought the tub full of water was just for him to take a bath. Of course, that would have used up all the water that others needed to shower with, but then he saw the goldfish. Jake came out of the bathroom and asked me what the goldfish were doing in the tub, so I had to explain to him how we showered in Indonesia. He got it and the goldfish remained safe.

While Jake was in our home, he tried to convert my entire family to Christianity. He even told me that he couldn't marry me, unless I converted to his belief. I wasn't going to change my faith, just because I wanted to marry him. To me, faith is a commitment to God and isn't something to be taken lightly. You can marry and divorce anytime you want to, but a commitment to God lasts forever. I therefore decided to let Jake go and live my life in Indonesia.

"FAITH IS A COMMITMENT TO GOD, PLEASE DON'T TAKE IT LIGHTLY"

After a couple of weeks in our house, Jake asked my mother if he could marry me and take me to America. My mother politely refused his request and told him that I needed to finish school. Jake tried to convince my mother that it would be even better for me if I finished high school in America. However, my mother was a very smart woman, and she told Jake that I needed to finish my schooling in Indonesia. If he wanted to marry me, then he should consider living in Indonesia. My mother wasn't easily influenced by a sweet-talking American.

A cultural difference also created a misunderstanding about the marriage proposal. My mother was insulted because Jake talked to her about the marriage without his parents being present. In my culture, the man's parents came to the girl's parents, bringing gifts for both the mother and the girl, and then they asked for the girl. My mother knew how serious Jake was about me, and she would do anything in her power to keep me from marrying him and moving far away from her...after all, I was her baby girl.

"TO A MOTHER, NO MATTER HOW OLD HER DAUGHTER IS, SHE IS STILL HER BABY"

After Jake went home, my mother knew that we were in love, and she didn't like the idea of her daughter being so far away from her...especially in America. She knew that this could lead to marriage, so she started to hide the letters Jake sent me. I argued with her about my rights, but to no avail. I finally decided my mother knew what was best for me, and my life was truly in Indonesia with my family. It felt like life with Jake was only a dream or a fairy tale that just wasn't going to happen for me.

I would see the postman once in a while, and he would give me Jake's letters, or my nieces and nephews would get the letters for me. I tried to listen to my mother's advice and forget about Jake, but he was very persistent and never gave up, even though I didn't write to him. Jake showed his love and determination to pursue me, as he continued to write two or three times a month.

"YOU JUMP THROUGH HURDLES IN PURSUIT OF LOVE"

Chapter 4

A Decision That Changed My Life

Since my mother started blocking delivery of Jake's letters two years ago, I was only able to receive them here and there. Life has been good though, and I have been working, making my own money and supporting myself. I believe that God's hand was upon our relationship, because He had plans for our lives. He sees things from the beginning to the end, and He was working things out in the middle. My mother's heart finally softened, and she started giving me Jake's letters again.

We began writing to each other again as friends. In one of the letters, Jake mentioned that he was going to take four months off from work to travel to Southeast Asia, and Indonesia was one of the countries on his list. He told me that if I wanted to see him again, then he would like to see me too. As we had become friends again, I thought this would be nice. When I mentioned Jake's plans to my mother, she said it was okay for him to come to Indonesia, but he couldn't stay at our house. During Jake's first visit to Indonesia in 1981, he met an American couple who were missionaries to Indonesia. Jake had kept contact with them, and they welcomed him to stay at their house.

"TRUE LOVE NEVER DIES"

Jake called me at the office today, and he told me that he was coming to my house tonight. I could hardly wait until work was over, so I could go home and get ready to see him. I had mixed feelings about his coming. While I was excited to see him, I didn't know what to expect either, because our communication had been broken for two years. As far as our relationship went, I didn't have high expectations as to what would transpire. I could hardly sit still waiting for him!

Suddenly, I heard his voice calling my name, and I jumped out of my chair and ran to the door. When I opened the door, my heart leapt! There he was standing at my door...still as handsome as the first time I saw him! I wanted so much to just run over to him and give him a big hug and kiss, but I restrained myself from doing so. I opened the door, and in he walked, giving my mother a hug and kiss on her cheek. He turned around and gave me a hug. I was very happy with the hug. For a few hours, we talked and caught up with each other, and then it was time for him to go. It was hard to see him leave, because I had missed him all those years. I still loved this man who had stolen my heart in 1981!

Jake stayed in Indonesia for 3.5 weeks, and he came to visit me every night. We both still loved each other, so it wasn't hard to pick up where we had left off in 1981. Since Jake wanted to talk with me alone, we decided to go for a picnic at the National Garden in Bogor. We took a train there and spent the day in Bogor. While we were picnicking, we talked about all the unanswered letters he had sent me, the broken communication and what we were going to do next. He finally said "I still love you and want to marry you. Will you marry me?" I answered "Yes!"

We talked about our career growth and when would be a good time to get married. Since both of us were changing jobs, we decided it would be best to give ourselves time to establish our careers. We determined that we would get married in March 1986, which would require my going to America. We also talked about the issue of my mother not approving of our being together, but we would cross that bridge when we got to it. I never said a word to my mother about Jake's proposal, but I figured that I had two years to work through that. Even though I loved Jake and wanted to marry him, I still had some doubt that he truly loved me and wanted to marry me after all those years of broken communication.

A few days later, Jake flew to Singapore to visit with a girl that he had met in Thailand while he was there. I was angry with him, although I accepted it. I couldn't blame him for wanting to see another girl, since I hadn't responded to his letters. In other words, I was cutting him some slack that I shouldn't have, especially when he had just proposed to me a few days ago. When Jake returned from his trip five days later, he came to see me and we talked. He told me that he wanted to make sure that I was the one he really wanted to marry, so I forgave him because I loved him.

"LOVE CAN BLIND YOU AND JUSTIFY ONE'S BEHAVIOR"

I changed jobs and became an executive secretary for a French company, which I really enjoyed. I did a lot of translation from Indonesian to English. Jake also changed jobs, but he was still in a computer-related job. During this time, we talked a lot about Jake changing his career from computer programmer to real estate agent. We decided that he would do real estate part time for now and see how it went, but still work his regular job. When we got married, I would help him in the business. Jake started working in real estate part time, and after a few months, he quit his job as a computer programmer and went into real estate full time.

Jake was still faithful about writing to me and I received his letters every day. He would call on weekends and we would talk for one to two hours. We were in love again and how good it felt! As March 1986 was approaching, Jake asked when I was going to come to America. Since it was winter, I said that I wanted to come in the spring when it wasn't so cold. I had excuses about the weather or my job to keep postponing my journey to America. Deep down inside my heart, I still doubted him, and the thought of him marrying me seemed like wishful thinking.

I remember it was a Saturday morning in April 1987, when the phone rang and it was Jake. He was very unhappy with me and all my excuses over the last year and a half for not marrying him, and he began to express his frustration about how patient he had been. Finally, he asked me a question that forever changed my life, "What do I need to do to make you come here?" Because I knew it would be impossible for him to come, I said to him, "Come and get me!"

Never underestimate the determination of a man in love! He asked, "What would happen if I came to Indonesia to get you and your family wouldn't let you go?" I replied that I would go with him. When he asked me again if I were serious about what I had just said, I answered, "Yes." Jake said he would call me again and hung up the phone. I just figured that he wouldn't come to Indonesia, and this would be the end of our relationship.

Boy...was I ever wrong! A few days later, Jake called and told me that he was coming to Indonesia and gave me his flight number. I was shocked and wondered what to do. How would I tell my mother that Jake was coming in ten days to take me back to America to marry him? It was like a dream.

"NEVER UNDERESTIMATE LOVE"

I knew what my mother was going to say, but I gathered up the strength and courage to talk to her about Jake coming to Indonesia. Of course, she wasn't happy and thought the idea was bizarre. She also knew I was an adult now, and I could marry the love of my life. There wasn't much she could say about it, but she would do anything in her power to stop me from going to America with Jake. It wasn't because she didn't like Jake as a person...she did like him. What she didn't like was the idea of her daughter living on the other side of the world where she wouldn't be able to see her very often.

That was the start of my nightmare! I felt like an unwanted person in my own home, as none of my siblings would talk to me. They were afraid of my mother and didn't want to be caught in the crossfire between me and my mother. I was glad I had a job that I could escape to during the day. Dinner at home meant eating alone. No one would talk to me, except my younger brother, who was hoping to talk me out of marrying Jake. Even though I previously doubted Jake, I trusted him now, because I saw how serious he was about marrying me. Jake was coming to pick me up, and that was enough for me to leave my family and go with him, which was the biggest decision of my life. I was ready to see what my life with Jake would be like. I guess the saying "love conquers all" was true.

On May 5, 1987, my brother and I picked Jake up at the airport.

We took him to the hotel, because my mother wouldn't let him stay in our home. Jake knew that his coming wasn't welcomed by my mother this time. When I told my mother that I was going to go to America with Jake, she was upset. Jake's plan was to stay in Indonesia for a week to talk to my family, and then he was going to whisk me off to America.

However, things didn't go as smoothly as Jake had planned, because my mother left home and went into hiding. It was a horrible ordeal with my mother for two weeks, because we were all worried about her. I later found out that she was hiding at my uncle's house, but no one wanted to tell me anything. Jake postponed his trip for another week, hoping we could find my mother and talk to her, but to no avail. My little brother scouted around hoping to find her with friends or relatives, but he had no luck. My mother had hidden herself, hoping it would deter my decision to go with Jake. I had to stay behind because I needed to find my mother, so I guess she had succeeded.

I took Jake to the airport and he was flying home to America alone; he even had to cancel our trip to Hawaii together. Before his departure, Jake handed me an airline ticket, and he told me that he had had enough of our roller coaster relationship and it couldn't continue this way. If I didn't make it to America by end of the month, which was May 1987, it would be the end of our relationship. He told me that if I decided not to go, then to cash the ticket in and send him the money. Jake left Indonesia without me.

I was numb and didn't know what to do, as my world was falling apart. Here was the love of my life giving me an ultimatum about my future with him. On the other hand, I had to find my mother and make peace with her. Of course, time was not in my favor, as it was close to a big holiday season in Indonesia. I decided to call the airline and have my name put on the waiting list to get on a flight to America. In the meantime, I managed to find out where my mother was. She had been hiding at my uncle's house, and she said she would come home in a week. I had to wait for her to come home, so I could talk to her. Life was difficult at home, as none of my sisters or big brother wanted to get into the middle of this matter between me and my mother. Just to get my mind off of the situation, I took comfort in visiting my girlfriends.

My mother finally came home, but she ignored me. When she did speak to me, it was always with harsh words. We finally did have that talk about my going to America, but my mother didn't agree with it. In fact, she told me that if I ever left the house, I couldn't come back and she would forget that she had ever had me. Those were the hardest words I've ever had to swallow, as my own mother said she would disown me if I married the love of my life. After that conversation, no one at home, except for my little brother, would speak to me. Furthermore, my mother took all of my jewelry, so I couldn't sell it. Luckily, I had saved some money from my salary before I had quit my job.

My little brother took me to visit my father at his home and we had a good talk. My father gave me his blessing to leave Indonesia and marry Jake in America. My father had also spoken with my mother, and he told her that she should bless me and let me go too. At least I had my father's blessing to marry Jake.

It was already third week of May 1987. I was calling the airline every day, but I was repeatedly told that my reservation was still on the waiting list. It was on the morning of May 27th that I received the phone call telling me that my reservation had been confirmed, and I could leave for America on May 30th. I told the girl on the phone to give my reservation to someone else, but she began to scold me. She had watched my reservation every day, and now that it was confirmed, she wasn't going to cancel it and give it to someone else. She told me that I had to leave on May 30th. Like a sheep, I listened to her and said okay.

I panicked after I hung up the phone, because I didn't have the money I needed to pay the exit tax. I have never left town, let alone the country, so I didn't know if I would need money to buy food or pay for something on the way. I made a collect call to Jake and told him that my reservation had been confirmed, and I needed money to leave the country. I didn't have a credit card, and the money I had wasn't enough to pay the exit tax.

Jake made a phone call to his missionary friend in Indonesia, and they loaned me $200 to pay for the exit tax. My friend Rebecca loaned me $100 to have in my pocket. I left home with a small suitcase and only a few clothes. Jake told me not to bring too much, because he would buy me things once I was in America.

On the morning of May 30, 1987, I left my home to fly to America. My brother and my cousin took me to the airport and said goodbye. It was hard to leave my home, but I also had peace, because I knew in my heart that my life in America would be okay. So, here I am, off to America by myself and I had met the deadline. I arrived in America on May 31, 1987 at 6:00 AM.

"TRUE LOVE WITHSTANDS TRIALS AND TEMPTATIONS"

Chapter 5

Challenges of Life

Here was I in America…all alone in a new country that I had never dreamt of stepping foot in. This was my country now where I would live with the love of my life, but did I really know him? Did I know his family? Did he really love me? Did he want to marry me? I didn't really know what was going to happen, but I did know that I loved him. Jake had given me the strength I needed to leave my family and country behind. I knew this man through his myriad of letters and phone calls, but I had only seen him three times in the seven years that we wrote to each other. Would love be enough for me to risk everything to be with him? These questions kept running through my mind, but I knew there was no turning back once I stepped out of my family's home and left for America. I guess the sayings "love conquers all" and "love is blind" truly applied to me. My only hope was our love for each other.

Through Jake's letters and hours of phone calls every weekend for the last three years, I felt I knew him pretty well, but I didn't know his family or have a clue about what his family was like. I knew how many brothers and sisters he had, but that was all. I truly did risk everything to be with Jake. As I looked back, I was always a risk taker and the one who calculated the outcome, whichever way it went. Somehow, there was a knowing in my heart that my life would be good with Jake, and I knew I would be okay in America.

"SOMETIMES YOU HAVE TO TAKE A RISK, SO YOU DON'T LIVE WITH THE WHAT IF'S"

I was tired, jet lagged and hungry. Jake and his parents picked me up, and he decided that I should stay with his parents until we got married. I was just okay with that, because I didn't have much choice in the matter, as my life was in his hands now. I didn't know anybody or anything about America, so I would just have to go along with whatever he said. I trusted him with my life, and I fully trusted that he was going to take care of me.

What a shock everything was! The weather was cold, even though the sun was shining, and it was light out until 9:00 PM. I had never experienced that before in my life! Where I came from, the sun would set at 6:00 PM and it got dark by 6:30 PM. The food here was terrible, very bland, and I couldn't eat it without Tabasco sauce. I finished a bottle of Tabasco sauce in three days! Speaking of the rice, it was different than what I ate back home; this rice cooked in 15 minutes and it didn't taste like the rice I ate back home. I missed everything about my country: the food, the people, the weather, but most of all, I missed my family, and I wondered if my mother missed me. I asked Jake to call my mother and tell her that I had arrived safely. I didn't dare to make the phone call, as I knew my mother wouldn't talk to me. I was also very uncomfortable, because I didn't have clothing warm enough for the weather. I had only brought summer clothing, which was pretty thin. According to Jake's family though, the weather was nice, but to me…it was cold!

I stayed with Jake's parents, and he would visit me when he was done working. We would go out to dinner or for a drive, and he then would go back to his house around 10:00 - 11:00 PM. Jake took me to his house on the weekends, so I could spend time with him. It was a learning process for me, because everything was different…even the washer and dryer.

After a week in America, Jake took me to his office and introduced me to his colleagues. That was the day I started learning about real estate. I knew nothing, and I couldn't even follow the form when I called the county for information. Jake had a part-time assistant who was nice enough to explain things to me. The office environment was not at all conducive to learning, as we had to share a desk between the three of us. Luckily, Jake was always out on appointments, so I shared the desk primarily with his assistant. When she sat down, I would stand up. When someone next to Jake was not in the office, then I would have a chair to sit in. Somehow, I was okay with that arrangement, as we had talked about doing business together when we got married. I was there to help him.

After two weeks in America, Jake's mother wanted to know if Jake had given me a ring yet, but I told her no. The American culture was completely different from the Indonesian culture; I didn't know what to do, and I didn't want to ask Jake about a ring. On a Wednesday evening, Jake took me out for dinner at a restaurant. After dinner, he gave me a box that contained a beautiful engagement ring, which had been designed especially for me…it fit me perfectly! He asked me if I would marry him and I said, "Yes!" I was so happy that I had been given the ring, yet I was sad that I couldn't share it with my mother and the rest of my family. I really missed my mother and being able to talk to her.

Now the pressure was on, as Jake's mother kept asking us about when we were going to get married. The following weekend, while we were driving, Jake told me that we should probably get married on June 27th. We decided that if it fell on Friday, then we would get married on the 28th. When we got home, we checked the calendar and guess what?! June 27th was a Saturday, so that was going to be our wedding day!

"LIFE IS FULL OF SURPRISES, EMBRACE IT"

Now that we were officially engaged, and we had decided that we were going to get married on June 27th, the fun of looking for a new home began. Jake told me that he had to sell his home, because he needed the money for us to get married, and we would have to live in an apartment. From the stories that I had heard in Indonesia, people in America usually started out in apartment living when they first got married, because they couldn't afford a house right away. I told Jake that I wouldn't mind living in an apartment. Then Jake smiled and said the reason he was selling his twinhome was so that he could buy us a house.

I wondered what was wrong with his twinhome…it was certainly big enough, but he wanted to have something new for us. Because Jake was a real estate agent, he took me to see about 40 homes, but none of them were to our liking. We knew what we wanted, but we hadn't found the perfect one yet. We finally saw our dream home, so we put money down and built our first home together on a small lake. Life was perfect! It was like living in a storybook where the girl meets her knight in shining armor and they live happily ever after!

The big day finally was here…June 27th, 1987. It was a small wedding attended by family and friends. I wore a simple dress that Jake's mother had bought for me, and I walked down the aisle escorted by his roommate. We had put the wedding program together ourselves, and we made our own version of the vows. When we said our vows before God, we promised that we would be there for each other through thick and thin, rich or poor, health and sickness till death do us part. We had the reception in our own backyard and the food was catered by a local eatery. We had Chinese food and the wedding cake was perfect! Jake's mother was kind enough to make arrangements for everything, and I believe they had paid for our wedding too. For that, I am forever grateful to her! Jake's mother helped me with my wedding when I didn't know what to do in a new country and I had no relatives here to help me.

"NEW LIFE, NEW JOURNEY ~ EMBRACE IT WITH PASSION"

Chapter 6

Building a Business Together

We are officially married now. While we waited for our home to be built, I moved in with Jake at his twinhome. We didn't really have a honeymoon; the only honeymoon we had was a night spent at a hotel downtown. We came home the next day, and we were back working in the office again on Monday morning. When we got married, I thought we would go somewhere on a honeymoon for a few days, but I guess that wasn't the case with us. As we were in the process of building our home, it didn't bother me at all. I guess I would rather have a home than a honeymoon, as we could always go on a honeymoon later.

I continued going to the office with Jake, sharing a desk with his assistant. Because she was getting married and moving away, Jake's assistant quit a month later. Now the responsibility of helping Jake fell fully into my lap. I was learning about the real estate business pretty fast, except when I made phone calls to the county. The clerk spoke too fast, and I couldn't find the areas on the form fast enough that needed to be filled in. I had to call two to four times, before I could get all the information that I needed. Jake would drop me off at the office in the morning, and I would do all the paperwork for him, while he would go for appointments either showing buyers homes or listing appointments. I had officially become Jake's assistant.

Two months after we were married, my period was late, and I was so scared that I didn't want to tell Jake about it. I remembered how my mother had cursed me, so that I would have had a hard labor. I was more afraid of my mother's curse than I was of telling Jake that I was pregnant. When Jake wasn't home, I would do jumping jacks. After two weeks, I finally got my period. I was relieved, yet sad at the same time, but I never told anyone about it. From that time on, I was very careful so that I wouldn't become pregnant. It just wasn't time to start a family yet.

I immersed myself in work as much as I could, so I wouldn't miss my family in Indonesia. One day, I gathered up the courage to call my mother and tell her that I was married now. She picked up the phone, we talked and everything was fine. She told me that she didn't want me to leave for America, because she was afraid that she wouldn't see me again. Jake had been very kind though, and he assured my mother that he would bring me home later in the year to visit. During our conversation, my mother told me that she had blessed our marriage. I finally had her blessing, and I cried after the phone call. That was a huge relief for me, because I could call my mother and talk to her now. I was connected to my family again and everything was fine!

"SOMETIMES WE WORRY ABOUT THINGS, BUT EVERYTHING IS FINE IN THE END"

I was young and naïve, yet I knew my duty as a wife. I hadn't integrated into the American way of life yet. Things were so different where I came from, and I was still learning the culture. Transportation was difficult, as Jake had to drop me off at the mall or grocery store. I had to wait until he was done with his appointments for him to pick me up. Many times, I would be waiting outside of a closed store, because he was running late with his appointments.

"MARRIAGE IS NOT GIVE AND TAKE...YOU GIVE A LOT MORE THAN YOU TAKE"

I learned very quickly that people don't go to the grocery store every day like I used to in my country. We bought a few packages of chicken at a time and froze them. It was a huge adjustment for me, because I was so used to going to the market and getting fresh meat, vegetables and fruit daily.

Another adjustment that I had to make was paying for everything with checks. Where I came from, everything was paid for with cash; checks were only used for business purposes. Jake, of course, didn't give me money to go grocery shopping, he gave me a check. The check only had his name on it, so I had to explain to the clerk that I just gotten married and it was my husband's check. They looked at me strangely, but they accepted his check. I went to the same grocery store every time, but I still had to give the same explanation. After a few months of this, I asked Jake to give me cash to go grocery shopping instead. Jake finally put my name on his account, so I didn't have to keep explaining my newlywed status to the grocery clerks. Jake talked to his mother before he added my name to his account, and she thought it was a good idea...she understood.

A few months later, we moved into our new home and got settled. We also moved the office, and now we worked at home, instead of going to an office that was about 25 miles away. I am getting used to my new role as a wife and I was doing my best to be a good wife. Jake was good to me.

We continued working together and Jake worked a lot of long hours. I understood the nature of the business, and I helped with everything that I could. I knew what a family business was like, as my family owned a coffee business, and we used to make the bags for the coffee.

We made a good team. Jake was the one on the frontline, and I was the person working behind the scenes, making sure everything was running smoothly. I'm used to working hard, so that wasn't an issue for me. I loved helping him. As for me, we were building our future together, and it was my duty as a wife to help him in any way that I could.

"TWO IS BETTER THAN ONE; A TEAM BRINGS MORE SUCCESS"

A few months later, we adopted a dog. Jake had always wanted a Chinese Shar-Pei, so we got one and named him "Beijing". This was the first dog that I had ever had in my life, so I didn't know what to do with one. Jake told me what to do with Beijing and I did as I was told. Soon enough, Beijing and I were inseparable. This was our first dog together and we still have very fond memories of Beijing. He was such a smart dog and he really knew his money! For example, if you put three $1 bills and one $5 bill in front of Beijing, he would always choose the $5 bill. We could also put two $5 bills and one $20 bill in front of him, and he would go for the $20 bill.

He always knew which one was the largest amongst the bills he was shown. When we had to put him down, it was the saddest day of my life. He was a very good dog and I still miss him.

A few months after we moved into our new home, I met Cris who lived two doors down from us. She was a stay-at-home mom with two wonderful children. Cris would call me and we would have coffee and cookies together. She was my first friend in America and she made me feel very special.

When I looked back, I realized the mistakes that we had made. We were more like business partners than husband and wife, because we immersed ourselves in building the business instead of our relationship. We spent a lot of our time together and saw each other every day, but the business was our main focus. Our relationship was more of a boss and assistant relationship. We didn't know how to nurture the relationship between husband and wife. We neglected us.

I believe that working together as a couple in a family business will always work, as long as your relationship is the first priority above the business. By filling your daily planner with things to do as a couple (i.e., going out to dinner, movies, the kid's ballgames, dance, recitals, etc.), your relationship will have a better chance of success, and so will working together. Another tip: No more talk about business once the office is closed. The mistake we made was to let the business control our lives, and our relationship became more about the business. After a while, where we started out as a married couple was lost.

"BALANCING MARRIAGE AND WORK IS AN ART"

Chapter 7

The Family We Dreamed Of

We continued working together and the business was growing, increasing by twenty percent each year. Life was good. We worked hard and we played hard. We took a vacation once a year and we would usually go where the water was beautiful. Every August, we would take out the World Atlas and look for the tiniest island; then we would call the travel agent to find out about the island and how to get there. We have been to many places and have enjoyed the beauty of God's creation. We appreciated the hard work we did throughout the year, so we treated ourselves to a nice vacation. Jake would also go out of town for conventions and seminars, and sometimes I went with him and enjoyed these mini vacations.

When you have your own business, and you are the rainmakers, you can't both go out of town for any length of time without difficulty, as there's no one to do your work for you. I was usually the person who kept things going, while Jake was away on business. I didn't mind that, as I understood the nature of the business…and after all, it was a family business.

When we got married, we agreed that we would wait five years before we would have any kids. That way, we would be established and having kids wouldn't be burdensome. As I looked back, the wait had been good for us, as it took us a few years to establish the business.

Two years after we were married, on one of our many phone calls, my mother asked me why I hadn't gotten pregnant yet. I told her that we wanted to wait to have children. I finally broke down crying, and I let her know about the curse she had put on me before I left for America. I also told her about what had happened, after we were married, when my period was late. My mother felt very badly, and she told me that she never intended to curse me. She was trying to scare me because she didn't want me to leave. Then she said, "I take it back! Now you can get pregnant and be fruitful." I was relieved and I felt like something had been lifted off of me. I was now free to have children, because my mother had blessed me.

Jake went to Las Vegas for a convention, while I stayed home to tend to the business. He was coming home today, and I was so excited that I could hardly wait to go to the airport to pick him up. As usual, he told me about the convention and who got what awards this year. Jake always made it into the top 20 of the company, so he came home with an award also.

"DON'T LET WORK OR BUSINESS CONSUME YOU; PRIORITIZE YOUR LIFE AND STICK WITH IT"

As soon as we got home, Jake told me that he felt the time was right to have a baby. I was surprised, as having a baby hadn't come up in our conversation for a while. He told me that while he was talking to a colleague at the convention, the subject of family came up. This woman had put a lot of time into the business, and she was telling Jake she regretted not having pursued a family earlier, because now she couldn't have a baby. Jake told me that he didn't want that to happen to him, and he felt he was ready to raise a family.

I always wanted to have a baby and now my dream was coming true. We were going to have a baby and raise a family. I was happy, but not excited about the news. In fact, I was numb. I would have been in a different emotional state, if I weren't mourning the loss of my father. A month ago, my father had passed away, and I was still grieving his passing. I went back to work, so I didn't have to think about my father, and cried.

"LIFE IS FULL OF SURPRISES, EMBRACE IT WITH A SMILE"

We tried for six months and I hadn't conceived yet. We decided that we wouldn't get stressed out waiting to conceive, so we determined to just let it happen when the time was right. We thought a break from the business and a vacation would be great for us, so we decided to join our company on a cruise to the Caribbean.

Well, it was a fun trip for the first two days. We were having a great time, when suddenly I developed a pounding headache that wouldn't go away. I was so sick that I couldn't leave the room. Jake made an appointment for me to see the ship's doctor, as I couldn't lift up my head. I wasn't seasick; I just had a pounding headache that was excruciating. I was going to see the doctor at 3:30 PM and there was a captain's dinner at 7:30 PM.

I made it to the doctor's office and he asked me a few questions. I answered his questions and then told him to just give me anything that would get rid of the headache. He said he couldn't give me anything until he did a pregnancy test. I thought that was ridiculous, since I only had a pounding headache, but I complied because I wanted some medicine. He came back a few minutes later and showed me the pregnancy test. I told him it was negative and to just give me some medicine. He said that it looked positive to him and he would give me some Tylenol. I was so surprised that I had to look at the pregnancy test again…and yes, it was positive! I was pregnant! The doctor gave me Tylenol and I felt better. I told Jake the news and he was very happy. That night was the most beautiful captain's dinner for both of us.

"CHILDREN ARE BLESSINGS FROM GOD"

A week later we came home from the cruise and we were sky high with the news of the pregnancy and the fact that we were going to have a baby. Jake called his parents to tell them that we were expecting a baby. I was apprehensive about how the news would be received by his parents, as I knew his mother wouldn't approve of us having a baby.

Jake's mother was always cordial to me in front of Jake, but whenever I was alone, she would call me and tell me things. I was right…she called me when Jake wasn't home, and she told me that I had made a mistake by becoming pregnant. I told her that it was her son who wanted a family. You see, his mother never really liked me. I overheard a few conversations between her and Jake about our marriage. She felt that I married Jake for a green card, and she was always trying to figure out what was wrong with me. She diagnosed me as having anything from PMS to a multiple personality disorder to bipolar disorder. In the beginning, she suggested that Jake should have our marriage annulled. She also said that he should either send me back home or pay me to leave the marriage.

If I had married Jake for a green card, then I would have left as soon as I had gotten it. I wouldn't have invested my life and energy into helping him build his business and loving him with all my heart. I always felt like an outsider with his family. I felt like they accepted me at an arm's length, but never really embraced me fully into the family. I was starving for love and being with a family. Although my family wasn't perfect, we were close, and I always felt loved by my family. When I came to America, I felt like I had been uprooted, but I was never really planted into his family. I believe they had some reservations about me marrying their son, and they wondered what my motives were. I had no motives, other than my love for Jake. I left everything in my country behind, and I got on the plane and came to America to be with Jake. The only thing I had was our love and I risked everything just to be with him.

"UNLESS YOU TAKE A RISK AND LOVE, YOU WON'T EXPERIENCE WHAT LOVE IS"

The pregnancy went very well. I didn't have any morning sickness; I just craved food. I was able to work at the office full time, going about my usual day. Cris, my best friend, was very happy that I was pregnant and she hosted a baby shower for me. I was involved in our monthly Bunco game in the neighborhood, so Cris invited all the ladies in the neighborhood to come. It was so wonderful to be surrounded by this circle of friends!

Nine months later, I gave birth to a beautiful baby, a son named Michael. He was tiny at 6 lbs 8 oz. The labor was 18 hours, but it was the happiest day of my life. We had a baby! My mom came to America and stayed for two months to help me with my baby, and she also brought me a nanny.

Since we worked from our home office in the basement, it was nice and very convenient for me to go upstairs and see my baby. The nanny would take care of the baby during the day, and at night, I resumed my duty as a mother. I would get up, nurse the baby and change him, and Jake woke up every night to make Michael a bottle. On the weekend, Jake would feed the baby and let me sleep in. Life was good as I juggled between work and motherhood…I loved every minute of it! The nanny quit after 1.5 years because she was getting married. I was now pregnant with our second son. We named him Daniel. I thank God for my sisters who came to America to help me for two months.

Life was good. The children went to a daycare a few houses away from ours, and two of my lovely nieces came to live with us for a couple years. It felt so good to have my family here with me… at least I no longer felt alone. We had fun together, as we juggled between the office, housework, and kids. And of course, we had some fun times at the mall!

As I looked back on my life, I realized that ever since I stepped foot in America, God has taken care of me completely. He has always provided for my needs. My family visited us and stayed for a while, when I couldn't make the trip home. When I was away from my family, He also gave me friends who filled the empty space in my heart…I was never alone!

"FRIENDS ARE THE FAMILY YOU CHOOSE"

Chapter 8

My New Found Faith

We were living the American dream. Life was good, business was growing by leaps and bounds and our family was growing too. The children were two and four years old by now; they were very good and smart. I worked at the office and my nieces helped me; we were a team. We had a very busy household and I thought I had it all. I was living out my dreams of having a happy family, growing the family business, and now that I finally had my family with me, I wasn't feeling as homesick.

I got pregnant again for the third time and I was hoping to have a little girl. I wasn't sweating it though, because it didn't really matter to me what I had, as long as the baby was healthy. As the family grew, I began thinking about our future and how I would like it if Jake spent more time with us. I didn't want to see Jake working that hard anymore, and I wanted him to spend more time with the kids, as they were getting older.

Because I was doing the bookkeeping for the business, I knew how much money we could save, and I had calculated what we would need to live comfortably. As you can see, I loved to play with the numbers and watch the money grow. I presented a plan to Jake about working smarter and saving more, which would give us options, allowing us to do what we love in life and spend more time with our family. Instead of him agreeing with me, he thought I was trying to prevent him from being successful. He told me that my plan would hold him back, so he fired me and hired a personal assistant.

I guess that didn't go very well. Not only did he fire me, but he also wanted to divorce me while I was pregnant. I felt like the rug had been pulled out from under me. I had given my life to him, and I was dedicated to helping him succeed in the business and with raising our family. Not only did I put my life on hold for him, I also gave up my dreams. I felt like a boat in the middle of the ocean just floating with no direction. My life was crumbling, but I didn't know what to do about it. I didn't have an identity other than being a wife and an assistant to Jake, which was the only world that I knew.

I didn't have a support system of friends who would come alongside me to help. Thank God my two nieces were here! They became the pillars that held me up, and even though they were falling apart themselves, they tried to be strong for me. My mother-in-law told me to give up custody of my children, because I wouldn't be able to afford to keep them.

Through all of this, we had a good friend named Mike who would call and talk to me and Jake. He had been our friend for many years; in fact, we had our first baby within one month of each other. Mike knew both of us and saw what was happening, but he never said anything to me, as he thought it wasn't his place. During this difficult time, Mike gave me some very good advice. He said that I should just enjoy being home, raising my kids without being involved in the office. There were a lot of women who would like to stay home and raise their children, but they couldn't. He felt that I should take advantage of this situation, as the children were getting older and needed more attention, plus I was pregnant with the third one. I knew that I didn't have any options, so I had to accept reality. I was used to being at the office, it was my world; but now, I was nothing and the thought of just doing nothing drove me crazy.

In the meantime, I went to counseling because it was hard not going to work at the office. My counselor was a good woman, she knew what was happening, and she gave me some good advice. Because the stress was too much for me, the counselor said that she could prescribe an anti-depressant for me. I refused the medication, because I was pregnant, and I was never keen on taking prescription drugs anyway. Jake was kind enough to let the kids go to daycare, which gave me time alone to rest.

Jake didn't remove me completely from the office work. I was still involved, but not with the daily routines. I still did the bookkeeping, paid the bills and checked the mail. At least I felt I was doing something.

During those days, I would wake up in the middle of the night, and I would just curl up in the bathroom and cry out to God for help. The pain was too much too bear. I didn't cry much in front of my nieces, so they wouldn't be concerned about me. Jake still lived with us, but his plan was to leave after Christmas. I asked him not to, because my nieces were planning on going home after the baby was born. If he waited until they left, then I wouldn't hold him any longer. If my nieces knew that Jake was going to leave me, they have been upset and worried about me, and they wouldn't have returned home. Jake agreed to stay until my nieces left. I was just going through the motions of life. Did I get depressed? I might have, but I still got up in the morning, got my children ready for daycare and cleaned the house.

"WHEN YOU THINK NO ONE HEARS YOU, GOD HEARS EVERY WORD YOU SAY"

I would call my mother and talk to her, because she was a very wise woman. She didn't tell me to get divorced or to stay in the marriage, but she did say, "In marriage, there are always temptations and trials, and that's when your love and faith are tested. How strong your faith and love are, will be the outcome of your marriage". What she said that day resounded in my ears and gave my heart some peace. I realized that I was going through some trials in my marriage, and how strong I was in weathering the situation would be the outcome of my marriage. I wasn't planning on getting married to get divorced. I thought if I could weather this, then I would be okay on the other side of this agony.

"TRIALS AND TEMPTATIONS IN YOUR MARRIAGE ARE TESTS OF YOUR LOVE AND FAITH"

During this hard time, a pastor helped and counseled us. The pastor called me into his office one day, just because he wanted to meet with me. At this meeting, he told me that when God made me, He had put a hole in my heart that only Jesus could fill. I looked at him with unbelief and one of those "yeah, right" looks. The pastor never tried to push me into getting saved or anything. He left it open for me to make my own decision.

I remembered going to church, and I kept going to the altar to give my life to Jesus. I made a deal with God…I told Him that

I would follow Him if He would fix my marriage. As soon as we left the church, we would fight on the way home. Then I would tell God that the deal was off; He didn't fix my marriage and we had a fight instead. This happened several times, and the pastor must have wondered what I was doing week after week. Jake finally asked me what I was doing, because I was going to the altar every time there was a salvation call. When I told him what I did, he said I couldn't do that. I told Jake the deal was off anyhow in my mind.

God knows everything; nothing is ever hidden from Him. He took note of my crying out for help and the deal that I was trying to make with Him. He didn't save me right away, nor did He fix my marriage according to what I thought it should be, but He did make everything easier for me from that day on. I couldn't say that life was back to normal, but the days were bearable now. I didn't cry as much, as I was adjusting to life at home, and I was still doing some work for the office, which helped my mind not go crazy. I would clean the house and do laundry, just to keep myself busy.

"WHEN NOTHING IS LEFT, THE ONLY WAY TO LOOK IS UP"

Because of the stress, the baby dropped and I dilated. When I was six months pregnant, the doctor ordered bed rest, which she said was necessary if I wanted to have a healthy baby. There was no way that I would jeopardize my baby, so I succumbed to bed rest even though it was difficult. I was an active person, so just being in bed all day and night didn't thrill me at all. I would get up and do the laundry and dishes, but I wouldn't lift anything heavy, as I had to take it easy too.

Jake changed his mind and decided not to divorce me. He said that we had weathered a lot in our marriage, and this was just another big hurdle that we had to make it over. I was numb with all that was happening. I was just surviving through the day and trusting God with the outcome. I have always had faith in God, which was something that my mother had instilled in all of us. She taught us to have faith in God because He always hears our prayers. She also said that God isn't blind; He sees it all.

In March 1997, David was born, but he came three weeks early. My nieces left two weeks after David's birth, so now it was only me, the children and Jake at home. The two older boys continued to go to the daycare in our neighborhood.

I went into post partum depression. I would just sleep during the day and only got up when I had to give David a bottle. David was a very good baby…the best of three. He was so cute, with a round face, big eyes and dimples that would melt your heart away. I would be in bed until 3:00 PM, and then I would get up, take a shower, pick up my kids from daycare, and cook dinner. This continued for several months. Jake would come home during the day to check on me. He knew I wasn't well and depressed, but he couldn't help me. I was numb and in survival mode. He would take me out on the weekend to run errands with him, just to get me out of the house.

I felt like my world was falling apart and I blamed Jake's assistant for my nieces returning home. I felt all alone with no one to talk to, but God always had a way to help. I had a best friend whose mother-in-law was an angel to me, because she knew that I was going through difficult times. My friend called and talked to her mother-in-law, and she drove from the city to my house. Bless her heart!

Grace was her name and it fit her very well. Grace came to my house and stayed with me for a few hours. She let me cry on her shoulder for hours and was just there for me. Her presence that day was like rain on a hot summer day. She made me feel better, as

I missed my mother, and she told me that she understood how I felt. From that day on, I felt better and better. Sometimes, you just need someone to encourage you and nudge you in the right direction. Yes, we all need someone to stand by us and show us that it's all going to be okay.

I would get up now in the morning and pick up the house, and I started opening the drapes and letting the sun in. As I was cleaning the house, I would sing "Amazing Grace", even though I only knew a few lines. I would repeat the song over and over again, and I would feel like raising my hands and praising God. I thought that was weird, because I wasn't a Christian, so why was I doing that? This continued for a few months, and I just thought that I was getting a bit out there with all of this.

The older kids were going to daycare and preschool and I only had the baby at home. I began wondering what I wanted to do with the time I had on my hands, so I started watching TV and learning about the stock market. I did this for a few months before I decided to trade stocks, because I always enjoyed watching money grow. In the meantime, life was getting better for me. I felt like I had a purpose now that I was getting up in the morning to watch the stock market on TV.

In December 1997, when Jake was on a business trip to Phoenix, Arizona, he asked me if I would go to a meeting hosted by a pastor from Missouri. He wanted to know about the pastor's message and he couldn't go, so I told him I would go and take notes for him. I arranged for a babysitter to come and watch the children. Nothing was going right that day, the children were crying and didn't want me to go, and the babysitter came late. The meeting was at 7:00 PM, but I didn't leave home until 7:00 PM, and there was freezing rain. I thought about not going and just staying home. But there was a tug in my heart to go, and I was told it was okay to keep going…and the rain just stopped.

"JUST LIKE THE WIND, YOU NEVER KNOW WHEN GOD MOVES"

I arrived at the meeting half an hour late, but I listened to the pastor, and took notes. He was quite interesting to listen to, and at the end of his meeting, he gave an altar call for people to get saved. I thought about how I had gone through this so many times, yet nothing had changed for me. Something inside me woke up that night when he said, "If something happens, no matter what, children will go to heaven, how about you?" What he said hit my heart… if my children were going to be in heaven, then I wanted to be in heaven with them. If the only requirement was to give my life to Jesus, then I would do it.

For the first time, I stood up and gave my life to Jesus without trying to make a deal with God. I said the salvation prayer. When I sat down, the guy who was sitting behind me tapped my shoulder to congratulate me and told me to find a church. Nothing significant happened that night. Jake called me later to see how the meeting went. I told him that I took some notes and I gave my life to Jesus. He was happy and crying. He told me that he had been praying for me all these years. As a matter of fact, he told God not to let him marry me, if I would never become a Christian. God answered his prayers…I got saved.

"GOD KNOWS EVERYTHING ABOUT YOU, NOTHING IS HIDDEN"

You see, those nights when I woke up in the middle of the night crying out to Him, He heard me. When I was making a deal with God, He heard my prayers. He knew that if He answered my prayers then, I would have said thank you and my life wouldn't have changed. God waited for the perfect moment to draw me closer to Him. He answered my prayers by making my days easier, and He carried me through my darkest hours, even though I didn't know it. At the right moment, when I was ready and willing to follow Him without trying to cut any deals, He came and saved me. He knew that was when I wouldn't turn back, and I would follow Him whole heartedly. He made me and He knew me even before I was in my mother's womb.

"JESUS...DON'T LEAVE EARTH WITHOUT HIM"

Chapter 9

A Curveball Was Just Thrown My Way

I still felt empty inside and loneliness had set in, as my two nieces had gone home to finish their schooling. I didn't have time to just stare at the wall, because I had to take care of my baby and two older children. Life was slowly returning to normal. I kept myself busy by doing the bookkeeping for the office, checking the mail, taking care of the house and, of course, spending time with the children. I had learned how to trade stocks, so that kept me busy also. God knew exactly what I needed to fill the void in my heart, so He gave me several good friends to walk with me.

When I first came to America, I became very good friends with Rinto and Nike. They had been in my life for a few years now, plus Rinto and I both served on the board of directors for an organization. As long as I have known them, they were always very nice people with a heart to serve others, and they opened their home to anyone needing help or just fellowship. They never mentioned

Jesus to me or tried to convert me to Christianity. Whenever I talked to Nike about my home situation, she would smile, pat my back and say, "Be patient, just pray". Their lives were a testimony of their walk with God. Because they were so different from my other encounters with so called "Christians", I began paying a little more attention to Christianity.

I probably would have become a Christian sooner, if I hadn't encountered so many Christians whose actions were the opposite of their talk…in other words; they weren't practicing what they preached. I remember telling Jake that I would consider Christianity, if he could show me an example of one Christian who walked their talk.

"LET YOUR ACTIONS SPEAK LOUDER THAN YOUR WORDS"

When they found out that I had given my life to Jesus, they decided to open their house to me, and a couple of other friends who had just gotten saved, for a Bible study. I could bring my children to the Bible study, and Nike would watch my children and cook dinner, so we could all have fellowship together. They invited me to their church, which we attended for a few months, and I was baptized there. I also joined a Bible study at their church with Nike.

"A JOURNEY WITH GOD IS A JOURNEY OF LIFE"

My marriage was getting better and we didn't get divorced. We had a babysitter helping with the kids, so we could go out on date nights, but we spent our weekends with the kids. We were determined to make our marriage work, and we were slowly but surely making progress with some counseling.

The two older children were now in school; one was in preschool and the other was in kindergarten. At the children's school, I met Patty who was a very nice person and also quite bubbly. When she found out that I was a Christian, Patty decided that I should join the Bible Study Fellowship with her. Patty was persistent, and after a couple months, I decided to join the Bible study. I enjoyed it and that's where I learned the Bible from front to back. I was now going to two Bible studies. Because of the distance, I decided to quit going to the Bible study with Nike, but I also joined another Bible study at the church closer to my house. We started attending the church as well, which is where my baby, David, was dedicated. I enjoyed studying God's Word, so I was still attending two Bible studies. In my brokenness, He found me and saved me, and He made me very hungry for His Word.

"GOD HAS HIS WAY OF COMING INTO YOUR LIFE"

Sometimes things happen in our lives and we have no clue as to why they happened, but God knows. He is the Master Planner; He sees everything and nothing is hidden from Him. My life was good before I got saved; but after I got saved, I realized that I had something that no one could ever take away from me. I was like a hungry baby for His Word, and He was quenching my hunger and thirst. He brought people into my life to point me in the right direction and to help me walk with Him. I have never been alone; He has always been there for me. But I had been blind and I couldn't see Him, and I had been too busy to distinguish His still small voice from all the noise around me, so I didn't hear His invitation to come just as I was.

I believe we are never alone, as God always has His eyes upon us, watching over us. Look at the birds, the fields and the fish; all the animals are fed and the fields are taken care of. Look at the flowers of the fields, they flourish in the wild and their beauty is on display for all to see. We think the birds are singing to us, but they are actually singing their praises and thanksgiving to God for taking care of them. Every creature knows God innately, except for us. We tend to ignore God because we think we can take care of ourselves, which is true in many ways. Because God cared for me, he brought Tammy into my life, who was also my neighbor. She was a Godsend to me, bringing comfort to my weary soul. When Tammy found out that I had become a Christian, she started taking me to conferences and church meetings. My faith in God grew by leaps and bounds! I was so hungry that I would go to any meeting just to hear about God.

"TRIALS IN LIFE DRAW US CLOSER TO GOD"

When I got pregnant again with our fourth child, we were excited and yet nervous. We already had three boys, who we loved very much, but it would be nice to have a little girl. Jake wanted a surprise with the fourth one, as we had found out the sex of our three boys before they were born. This pregnancy though was very different from the others. The baby didn't move around as much, and when there was movement, it was more like the baby was stretching.

During one of the visits, the doctor asked if I had any concerns, and I told her that this baby didn't move around as much as our other babies had while I was pregnant with them. She ordered an ultrasound right away, and we found out that the baby was in the breach position at five months gestation. The doctor told me not to worry, because the baby would turn closer to delivery. Well, that wasn't the case, because the baby didn't turn, and the doctor prepared me for the possibility of a C-section. One of the doctors in the clinic was known as being the best at repositioning a breached baby, so we prayed and made an appointment on Monday.

Well...I guess this baby didn't want to be turned around. My water broke on Friday morning, and I had to have an emergency C-section at 36 weeks gestation. The room was full of doctors and nurses waiting for the birth of our baby girl. When she was delivered, she cried so loud that I knew she would be okay! We named her Kyle. She is a double blessing from God, as she was born on June 27, 2000, our wedding anniversary.

When Kyle was a week old, I gave her a bath, fed her a bottle, and laid her down in her bassinet in my bedroom. I was rubbing some herbs on my stomach, when I heard her cough. I went to the bassinet to check on her and she had just spit up. When I picked her up to change her, she breathed in the spit and was gagging. As the mother of four children, I knew what to do...so I tried tapping her on the back to clear any debris. When I saw that she was having difficulty breathing and tears were coming out of her eyes, I knew she was in trouble, so I called 911.

Within five minutes, the paramedics had arrived at my home. I ran downstairs with Kyle...I had forgotten that I had just had C-section. The paramedics shook their heads when they saw her. Somehow though, I didn't see any change in Kyle at all. I looked at the paramedics and asked them if they wanted to hold her...they looked at each other and one of the men said yes. He took Kyle from my arms, sat her up and started tapping on her back, while I called her name.

I quietly spoke to God saying, "You are not going to take my baby girl from me...come down from heaven and help her!" A couple minutes later, Kyle coughed and a big glob of stuff came out. The paramedics whisked her away to the hospital by ambulance. I later learned that Kyle could have had brain damage, due to the lack of oxygen. I thank God that today Kyle is a healthy, witty and smart young girl, who is full of life and determination.

"GOD GIVES YOU THE DESIRES OF YOUR HEART ACCORDING TO HIS WILL"

In everything there is a reason for a season. I learned everything that I could about God and His Word, and I was also learning about healing and deliverance. I went to every class or meeting I could find, and God always had someone there to take me where I could learn more. At that time, I didn't know that God was training me and building up my faith for what was coming. Life sometimes has its twists and turns, but we must be flexible enough to go with it; otherwise, we can be thrown off course. Yet, if we keep our eyes on Him, He is there to keep us on the right track or to reposition us when things go awry.

Two weeks before our family vacation to our timeshare in Cancun, Mexico, Jake got the surprise of his life. All of his staff and sales team quit, except for the office courier, which forced me back into the office to learn what was going on. I had time to mend the broken relationship that I had with Jake's office assistant, because I had blamed her for my nieces going home. She taught me a lot of new things about the office, as I hadn't been involved in the daily operations for four years. I was glad that I had the chance to apologize to her now, because I knew it wasn't her fault. She had worked for Jake for four years, and she was the best assistant we've had. Before we went on our family vacation, we had to close the office. After we returned, the plan was that I would fill in at the office, until a new assistant was hired, and I would do my book-keeping at home again.

Well, we can plan, but things don't always work out according to our plans. Jake wasn't feeling well and he had developed a cold that had lingered for six weeks. When he went to the doctor to get some antibiotics, he was jaundiced and there was a good possibility that he had hepatitis. Jake went through all the tests to determine what type of hepatitis he had, but the results were negative. The doctor told Jake that the jaundice would resolve on its own. I cooked all kinds of food for him to eat from salad to Jell-O to juicing, but he had no appetite at all. He did, of course, receive prayer and tons of it.

"TRIALS AND TRIBULATIONS ONLY MAKE YOU STRONGER"

After six weeks, Jake felt better, but he hadn't fully recovered and got tired easily. I knew he wasn't feeling well yet, and it was hard for him to rest at home, as we had four little kids and two dogs. One weekend, he told me that he just needed some rest, so he checked into a hotel near our home. The next day, Jake called me and told me that he was dizzy, so I picked him up and took him to the urgent care facility. The doctor there ordered a complete blood workup to see if the cause of the tiredness and dizziness could be identified in Jake's blood. When the doctor received the results of his blood tests, he told us that Jake was very sick, and he needed to go to the hospital right away. I took him to the hospital and checked him in.

The following day, I dropped the kids off at school. As I was driving home, I began a conversation with God about not knowing what Jake had and his hospital stay. When I came to a stoplight, I heard God say to me, "Lean on Me like you have never leaned on

Me before, and trust Me like you have never trusted Me before."

God had allowed this dark situation in my life, but I also trusted that He would carry me through it, so I said out loud to Him, "Alright then; You got me in and You get me out." That was the start of a faith journey of truly leaning on and trusting God through the valley of the shadow of death for us. Jake was diagnosed with Aplastic Anemia and the chance of survival was very minimal. We prayed and stood on the Word of God that He healed us. We changed Jake's diet; he juiced and underwent detoxification. We also had friends that rallied behind us and prayed.

"FAITH BELIEVES AND DOESN'T LET GO"

I had to run the office by myself through all of this, and I thank God for the courier and my niece, Veilya, who helped me after her schooling. When I went back to work fulltime at the office, I had to juggle between work, home, and the kids and their activities. I was able to manage it all though, because my work day was flexible. I could take time off during the day and work at night when the kids were sleeping. I also had a sister who helped me with my children. Everybody chipped in to help and I believe that's what a family should be about. I would work until 8 - 9 PM at night at the office, and then I would go to a revival meeting to get prayer for Jake.

When I was hit with fear, I would cry out to God, and within a few minutes, I got the strength I needed to accomplish what I had to do that day. God covered me with His grace. Looking back, I couldn't have done it without Him. I'll bet that I had angels surrounding and helping me day and night. I didn't worry about Jake's illness, because I knew God was going to heal him, and it was just a matter of time. Four months later, Jake was healed completely, and it was like nothing had ever happened to him!

A year later, we all went back to Indonesia to visit my family. It was the second time that Jake had visited my family in the 15 years of our marriage.

I thank God every day for His mercy and loving kindness. He is a good God! There isn't a day that passes that I don't think about God and how good He is to us. God gave us a second chance in life and I'm forever grateful to Him!

Chapter 10

The Struggles of Love

I was very close to my mother, so when she passed away the week before Christmas in 2005, I was devastated. It was difficult to get an airline ticket home that time of year, but God was so good me. I was able to get the last two remaining seats on a flight to Indonesia, so I asked Jake to go with me. Since I was going home to bury my mother, he declined and thought it was something that I should do by myself. Jake decided that he would rather take a vacation to our timeshare in Cancun with our two older sons than go with me. Everything happened so fast that I was numb and just going through the motions. Consequently, I went home alone for my mother's funeral. When my family asked me about Jake, I told them that he had business and the kids to tend to.

On the morning that she died, my mother had gotten up, eaten her breakfast and had gone over to the neighbor's house. While sitting on the terrace of our home after her return, she complained to my sister that she felt dizzy. My mother passed out and never regained consciousness…she was gone within 24 hours.

I was still in shock after the funeral and I would just sit and cry for hours. One of my sisters, Yulan, would come to the house and just sit in front of me and talk. She talked about anything under the sun, until I would engage in conversation with her and stop crying. Another sister, either Asen or Enang, would cook food and bring it to me, so that I would eat. I stayed with my family for three weeks in Indonesia and then I returned home.

Once I was home, I continued to cry and I couldn't remember what I did from one hour to the next. I would brush my teeth five times a day, because I couldn't remember if I had brushed my teeth or not…the only thing I did notice was that my toothbrush was still wet. This happened for another month.

I continually prayed, asking God where my mother was and one night I was given a dream. I was taken by a man in white clothing to a beautiful garden. He then pointed to a man in the distance and told me that it was the Lord. I ran to Him and we embraced. He took out something that looked like a camera, handed it to me and told me to look into it. When I looked through the view finder of this "camera", I saw my mother walking in the garden. When I woke up, I knew in my heart that she was in heaven. From that day on, I improved daily and I was able to return to work two weeks later.

"PRECIOUS IN THE SIGHT OF THE LORD IS THE DEATH OF HIS SAINTS"

Although your heart can stand still after life events occur, time has a way of marching on relentlessly, and months had passed. Life seemed to be back to normal and I thought everything was going great - the family was growing, and the business was doing very well. I was hosting conferences, which were becoming very successful, as the attendees grew from 25 to 1,000 in two years. I was on top of the world and I thought I had it all, until one evening when Jake handed me a letter to read.

I didn't have a good feeling when I opened the envelope that contained a three-page letter. As I read the letter, my heart was racing. I could hardly comprehend what I was reading, as I was in total disbelief. In short, Jake was asking me for a divorce. The letter was all about what I had done wrong, why he was unhappy with me, and how it would be better for us to go our separate ways. I was confused, because I didn't know where this was coming from or how it had reached this point. I thought our lives were good and he loved me...now what's wrong?

"LOVE CAN BE MANIPULATED BY SELFISHNESS"

I was in shock and I cried, as I felt the world spinning uncontrollably around me. I wanted to call my mom and hear her say that everything would be okay, but she was gone now, and I didn't want the rest of my family to worry about me. So instead, I called my best friend, Joy, who is like a big sister to me. Joy was very good to me, and she would pick up my phone calls any time of the day or night. It didn't matter whether it was at 4:00 AM or midnight... Joy was always there whenever I needed someone to talk to and her words comforted me. I thank God for Joy who walked closely beside me through this difficult time in my life!

I was having such a hard time one afternoon that when I called Joy to talk, she invited me to lunch. She lived 45 minutes away from me, but I decided to make the drive to her house anyhow. After lunch when we were sitting on her porch, Joy said something to me that was so beautiful that I won't forget it for the rest of my life. She said, "You don't need any drugs, I will hold up your hands just like Aaron and Hur did for Moses." And she was there for me through my divorce. I realized that our friendship had turned into sisterhood.

"A FRIEND IS SOMEONE WHO KNOWS THE SONG IN YOUR HEART, AND CAN SING IT BACK TO YOU WHEN YOU HAVE FORGOTTEN THE WORDS."

Joy recommended that I go for counseling and highly recommended her counselor. I felt that I needed counseling, because I needed someone I could talk to professionally for my own sanity. I was desperately grasping for words of hope that I could hang onto, so I called Joy's counselor. Jeanne was an older woman, and I began counseling with her three times a week. I needed someone to tell me that this was a bad dream and it would all be okay when I woke up.

The fact was that it wasn't a dream. My life and marriage were falling apart, and the reality of it took me totally by surprise…I never saw it coming. After all that we had been through with his health and the business, I thought we had grown beyond all this. I thought we were a team and we would be together to see our grandchildren until death parted us. A few friends told me that this storm would pass, as he was going through his mid-life crisis, and to give him time to get through it.

"BETRAYAL OF LOVE IS THE CRUELEST THING TO EXPERIENCE"

I still went to work at the office, but I didn't say anything to the staff. It felt good to work, as I could at least forget about what was happening in my life. I had clients that I needed to take care of and staff and bills to pay. Taking care of the children also helped me forget the problems I was facing at the moment. Jake withdrew from the family and he no longer joined us for dinner. When Jake came home, he would watch TV, or he would be on his computer, and he was constantly on his cell phone. There wasn't much communication between us. We still slept in the same bed together, but I would go to bed earlier than him.

Jake didn't want to go counseling, as he thought it was just a waste of time and money, plus he didn't feel that he needed it. In his eyes, the problem was me, and I was the one that needed counseling more than him. After talking to him about Jeanne and how she had helped me during these hard times, he agreed to go to counseling with me a couple times to explain to Jeanne what had gone wrong in our marriage. After the two counseling sessions with Jeanne, he agreed to go counseling with me once a week. Additionally, I would go to counseling two more times a week, as I needed it for my sanity.

Jake pulled away from me and the children too. My marriage was falling apart, and now I was having a difficult time with the two older boys. They were very angry with me, and they were constantly telling me that it was entirely my fault, and I didn't understand why. There was fighting on all fronts at my house, and it was very hard not to lose control of my temper. I later found out from my two older boys that Jake would take them to the health club to exercise and then out for dinner. He would tell them at dinner how unhappy he was with me, how miserable his life was and that he wanted a divorce.

"A MAN'S HEART IS DECEITFUL, WHO CAN UNDERSTAND IT?"

We continued to go to counseling, and I thought we were making progress, but the tension in the house was unbearable. Jake came home every day and slept in the same bed with me. I would pray for him and ask God to help me with my marriage. One thing that God gave me was the gift of sleep. No matter how difficult or dreadful things were, I could somehow compartmentalize those problems and sleep like a baby. God knew what I needed!

During dinner with some friends, Jake announced that he was going to Cancun with another friend for two weeks. That was shocking to me, because he hadn't told me anything about it. In his mind, he had already left, he was leading his own life, and he didn't feel that he had to tell me anything anymore. I knew I couldn't go with him anyhow, because all the children were in school and my daughter was in a church play, which was a commitment for the month of December.

December was a crazy month! I was very busy with the church play and trying to run the office while Jake was away on his vacation, plus tending our four children and the pets…and yes, there was Christmas to contend with too! The children weren't very excited about Christmas this year, as there were no presents under the tree. I would usually have the presents wrapped and ready by the time the tree went up, but not this year. When the children asked why there were no presents, I told them that they just hadn't been wrapped yet.

Jake came home from his vacation two days before Christmas, and we had a very nice Christmas as a family. The day after Christmas, the children said they were very surprised by the gifts they had received from us. I later learned from the children that before Jake left on his vacation, he let them know that there wasn't any money to buy presents with this year. I was angry because that wasn't what we had discussed about Christmas, plus I was mad that he had given me and my sister a set of three movies. While confronting Jake about Christmas, I blew up and told him to move out of the house.

I called my counselor, Jeanne, and explained to her what had happened. I guess I was mad about many things. I was mad about him going on vacation alone, and when he came back from vacation, he went to a Christmas party and never asked me to go with him. I wanted a separation, as I couldn't tolerate the coldness or his behavior anymore. On December 28th, he moved out of the house and stayed at our home office, which was across the street from where we live. We agreed to separate for six months and still go to counseling during the separation. It was also decided that I would have the kids Monday through Friday, and he would have the kids on the weekends.

"WHAT WE TOLERATE CAN KILL US"

I had never been separated from Jake before, except for those few times when I had gone home to see my family in Indonesia or whenever he had attended conventions…and his recent vacation. It was a hard decision for me to make, but I had to do it for my sanity and for the sake of the kids. I didn't want to feel the tension in our home anymore, as everyone was acting up; even the dogs were barking at every little noise they heard. It was currently a hostile environment, and I needed peace in my home, while we were working on our issues separately.

After the kids went to bed, I was checking emails on the computer. After an hour, I turned the computer off. As I was getting ready to go to bed, I heard that still small voice telling me to go back downstairs and turn on the computer. I thought that was funny, because I had just finished checking my emails. But I went downstairs anyhow and turned my computer back on, and the still small voice guided me to browse the Internet. I came across Jake's Facebook account and when I clicked on his friends, I saw pictures of women in their bikinis. I didn't like what I saw that night. I spent a few hours looking at his Facebook page and printing out pictures.

"TRUST IS LIKE AN ERASER, IT GETS SMALLER WITH EVERY MISTAKE"

The next day I called him and asked him to come to my house. When he showed up, I told him about the pictures I had found on Facebook and asked him what he had to say. Jake was calm and he told me those women were his friends on Facebook. He said he didn't know a lot of them, because some were friends of friends, and some had just become his friends on Facebook. Jake admitted to having had an affair, but it wasn't with any of those women. I thought the letter was the biggest surprise of my life…but the affair certainly exceeded that!

I was surprised by how calm I remained and that I could listen to what he was saying. Jake told me that the affair was with a girl from Turkey who I had met in 2006, and he had started writing to her shortly after our trip to Turkey. The affair had lasted two years and ended in May 2008, and I didn't even know that it had happened. Jake said it was over now and that he would tell me anything I wanted to know about the affair.

I was so shocked that I couldn't even think of one question to ask him. I didn't know what to do after his explanation…should I cry or scream? I was so oblivious to what had been happening in my own life! After he left, I called my counselor and talked to her about the affair. At her suggestion, Jeanne and I met, and she was able to calm me down with her words. I respected Jeanne and her advice. Because she was an older woman, it was just like I was talking to my mother. I missed my mother so much, and I wished that she was here to say that everything would be okay!

The betrayal of love is hard to swallow. I hated Jake for what he had done to me, but I still loved him so much. He was the love of my life…how could he do this to me? I trusted him with all my heart and I never thought he would cheat on me! He knows the Bible very well and what it says about adultery. It was like a nightmare that I couldn't wake up from.

"BETRAYAL IS THE ULTIMATE KILLER OF A RELATIONSHIP"

Chapter 11

Faith Carries Me Through

I continued to work at the office, but now the staff knew about the affair and our separation. They didn't take either side…they just prayed for us. While there was still tension at the office, it wasn't as much as it had previously been.

The kids began weekend visits with Jake, which didn't last very long. The first week, the kids could hardly wait to spend the weekend with Jake, and they brought the dogs with them. I left my house during that time, because I didn't want the kids to call or come home when they were supposed to be visiting their father. I thought it would allow some good bonding time for them, as Jake was always working late. The second week, they wanted to go over to his house later in the day on Saturday, and by Sunday afternoon, they wanted to come home sooner than the agreed-upon time. By the third week, I couldn't get them to go to their father's house across the street.

By the fourth week, it had gotten worse. I overheard the kids calling their friends and asking if they could sleep overnight at their houses. It broke my heart when my daughter, who was now eight-years old, called my best friend to see if she could spend the night at her house. I called Jake and suggested that it might be much easier for everyone, if he would just come over to visit on Friday nights. The kids wouldn't have to leave the house that way, and they could sleep in their own beds. I would leave the house and then he could take the kids out on Saturday. Jake agreed to this arrangement.

As our marriage was falling apart, the business got hit also. The real estate market slowed dramatically, and it was no longer business as usual. We had to follow the market trend of short sales, because a lot of homeowners were under water with their mortgages. Jake and I went to a real estate training class in Chicago on how to do short sales. Even though we were separated, I was still fully committed to my marriage and helping Jake with the business. After all, it was our livelihood and I thought this storm would pass too.

"SOMETIMES, YOU JUST HAVE TO RUN INTO THE EYE OF THE STORM TO FIND PEACE"

I loved Jake so much that I couldn't imagine my life without him. Even though I hated what he had done to me, I knew that I had contributed to the breakup of our marriage also. Our separation lasted for six weeks and then we started dating each other. I felt like a teenager again, when I would tiptoe to his house and spend the night there.

After three months, Jake would come home on the weekends and then go back to his house during the week. It was awkward, but we had agreed to separate for six months, until we had decided what we would do.

During the separation, there wasn't as much tension in the house, so it was easier for me to process things. I was now beginning to accept the reality that divorce was a possibility, because of my husband's emotional affair with a woman in Turkey. Yes, it was an affair, no matter what you wanted to call it. Some people thought an emotional affair was somewhat better than a physical affair, because there was no physical contact with the other person. However, most affairs begin with the emotional intimacy, which then leads to the physical kind, if they are in close proximity. To me, an affair is an affair…whether it's a full blown physical affair or an emotional affair, because it's a betrayal of love and trust. I found out that it was difficult to trust the other person completely after an affair. Trust is something that is easily broken but very difficult to rebuild.

Throughout this entire ordeal, I leaned on God and clung to Him as tightly as I could. He was the only one who could give me peace and cover me with His grace. Without prayer and counseling, I would have checked into a mental institution or would have required serious medication. It was God who pulled me through the darkest hours of my life.

"WHEN NOTHING IS LEFT, BEND YOUR KNEE AND LOOK UP"

Ever since Jake had handed me that shocking letter in May 2008, I had prayed and asked God to reveal to me where I had fallen short as a wife and what had gone wrong in my marriage. Since then, God has been taking me back in time and showing me things that I had been oblivious to, because I had loved and trusted Jake so blindly.

For two years, I had dreams that Jake was having an affair, and sometimes the dream was so real that I would cry in my sleep. When

I would tell Jake about my dreams, he would just brush them aside and tell me that I was just dreaming. In the last dream though, God showed me the woman that he had the affair with…she was an Asian with blond hair. I didn't recognize her at first, because her hair was brown when I met her in 2006. Since then, she must have dyed her hair blond.

"THE BEST PROOF OF LOVE IS HONESTY AND TRUST"

I felt like God was playing a slideshow in my mind, showing me things during the affair that I had been oblivious to in my daily life. Jake would go to a coffee shop to work, because he said the office was too noisy. He was constantly on his cell phone texting, even during dinner at home. Jake would watch TV, while he was chatting with her on his laptop. If I sat next to him, he would ask me to move; although I didn't read anything, because I thought he was working. When Jake showered, his cell phone was next to him. Then he put a password on his cell phone, which he had never done prior to the affair. On Saturday, when he said he was going to the health club, he was often at a pool party at a friend's house. I should have picked up on these clues, but I didn't because I trusted him. My love for him had actually blinded me to his behavior.

"LOVE IS BLIND"

My brother used to jokingly say to me, "Love is blind and when you're blind, you can't see. When you can't see, you crash". I used to laugh when he said that, but now I was living out the very saying that I had laughed about. There wasn't a hint of the affair, nor could I see any faults in him. To me, Jake was a good husband and father;

he was also faithful and hardworking, so I protected him. I did all the work, so he could rest and spend time with me and the children.

Without a doubt, my faith in God helped me through the struggles of life. I believe that from the moment Jake handed me that letter, through the separation and finding out about the affair, God had protected me. All the prayers of my friends, plus all the prayers that I had prayed, created a shield around me. These life events drew me closer to God, and I leaned on Him more than I can possibly imagine. God gave me abundant peace and surrounded me with His grace, as I passed through the darkest hours of my life. Additionally, God placed the right friends and counselor in my life precisely when I needed them to help me along the way.

"FAITH WILL SEE YOU ACROSS TO THE OTHER SIDE"

After six months of separation, Jake couldn't decide if he wanted to stay married or get divorced, so we extended the separation another six months, but this time he came home and lived with us again. We continued counseling once a week with Jeanne. I knew if I wanted the marriage to succeed, then I had to forgive him. In the meantime, Jake displayed a willingness to work on the marriage too. We were making progress in our relationship, and at the suggestion of Jeanne, we went on date nights. It was good to spend time with Jake; after all, he was my husband and I loved him!

"TRUE LOVE DOESN'T COUNT THE COST"

Chapter 12

Conquering the Beast

As we continued working on our marriage with counseling and by dating each other again, the business was improving also. The children were settling down now and there wasn't as much tension at home or in the office. I thought we were making tremendous advancement on the road to restoration.

As for me, I needed God to cleanse me and help me to release all the anger, bitterness, rejection, and resentment that I had held. In order for full restoration to take place, I knew that I had to genuinely forgive Jake. I continually asked God to show me the things in my life that had hindered me from being who He created me to be.

"LIVING IN BITTERNESS IS LIKE DRINKING POISON"

When you pray to God, He hears your prayers. And in response to my prayers, God began revealing things to me about my temper and how I had reacted to different situations. I didn't like what I was shown, when God allowed me see how I had interacted and responded to my children. I asked Him to remove that from me, which He did. I could relax more now, because I was no longer easily angered, and I had more patience with people in general, but especially with my children.

I was so blessed to have Jeanne as my counselor; not only was she wise, but she also prayed for us. Jeanne prayed for me many, many times, as she helped me walk through the valley of darkness. It was in that place that the Lord showed me things about myself that I didn't even know I had. He also revealed things to me that I knew I had, but I was previously unwilling to give up, although I knew that I had to.

Love really does conquer all. In my case, it was my love for Jake and my family, and the fact that God loved me, which caused me to want to be a better person. I was ready to give up all the junk in my life, so I could have the more abundant life that God had spoken about so many times. My prayer to God was for the restoration of my marriage; I earnestly desired that it would become a better marriage that was full of love, joy and peace.

"NOTHING IS BETTER THAN A HAPPY MARRIAGE"

In my walk with God and the restoration of my marriage, I realized I couldn't go halfway with Him. I had to willingly let go of all the hurts, unforgiveness, frustration, anger, bitterness, rejection and resentment. I had to release it all and never pick it back up again!

One of the hardest things to do is face the enemy and see the beast, knowing that it's within you. When you have the courage to see the ugliness of the dark side of your soul, you will also be required to release that part of your life. I have prayed hundreds of times, asking God to cleanse me. While He helped me with some of the big obstacles, He wouldn't completely cleanse me until I was willing to give up mentally and emotionally. He is a gentle God and He won't force Himself upon us. We have to voluntarily come to Him...and He is always there and waiting. When He showed me the impact of my behavior and the frustration it had caused my children, I was ready and willing to surrender to Him, because I didn't like what I saw. I felt that whatever it was that I carried then had to be stopped now, because I wanted my children to be happy. I didn't want them living in fear of when I would blow up at them again, because of the little things they had done wrong.

"IN EACH OF US, THERE IS A BEAST TO CONQUER"

You see, I had taken my anger and frustration out on them, without realizing the impact I had made in their lives. I was also sending them mixed messages. On one hand, they know that I love them very much and we have fun together. On the other hand, I would become very angry at the little things they did or the mistakes they would make. I love my children and I wanted to have a great relationship with them, but it had to start with me, and I was willing to let go of my junk and let God clean me up.

As we continued weekly counseling with Jeanne as a couple, I could see things were improving and we were able to release some of our frustrations towards each other. I continued asking God to show me the things that I needed to let go of emotionally in my life. As I was willing to surrender it all to Him, He began to show me the fear and anger, which had been deeply rooted in me since my childhood. And I thought to myself...now how could that be?

One night, when Jake and I had an argument, I stormed into the bedroom. As soon as I closed the door behind me, God started talking to me about how unhappy He was with my behavior, which He likened to that of a spoiled little brat. I stopped to think about the argument with Jake that I had just had a few minutes ago. And I realized that it was childish…I agreed with God that I was a grown-up woman and I shouldn't be behaving like a child.

Right away, I was given a vision of when I was about 7 - 8 years of age. In that vision, I saw my father whipping me with his belt, because I didn't have my shoes on when I went outside to play. He had warned me several times, but I didn't comply. My father didn't want me playing in the street barefoot, as I could get hurt stepping on broken glass or nails. I cried when I saw the vision, because I could feel the fear and anger as that little girl and I saw myself crying. I knew then that those were the two biggest strongholds in my life, and I asked God to heal me from fear and anger. I felt the cool breeze of God come upon me, starting at my head and then washing over me, and I felt so much peace. Suddenly I had another vision of the same little girl growing up and becoming an adult…it was me.

There was a part of me that hadn't grown up; it was stuck in time, where I was patronized by my father. Now I understood why I had acted like a little child. God has done some mighty works in my life emotionally, and that night he surgically repaired my heart, so a deep inner healing could take place. From that night on, my attitude changed and I starting acting like a grown-up woman…I no longer acted like a child.

Without God's love, patience and grace, I wouldn't be who I am today. Like an emerging butterfly, I have grown into the beautiful woman that He always intended me to be. I am just amazed at the

progress I have made! The key to my inner healing was my willingness to surrender it all and go all the way with Him. Even though
facing the beast was the hardest part of my inner healing, I have
conquered that beast by submitting myself to the Lord.

"THE ENEMIES OF FAITH ARE FEAR AND DOUBT ~ CONQUER THEM"

Chapter 13

What Just Hit Me Again???

As time went on, life was returning to normal and we were on the road to restoration. We continued our counseling with Jeanne every two weeks. Jake came home after a few months of separation, but he only brought home half of his clothes, leaving the rest at our home office. From time to time, I would mention bringing the rest of his clothing home, so he wouldn't have to change his shirts at the office, but Jake told me that he didn't mind changing there. It should have been a clue to me about his uncertainty, because he seemed to be more out than in for the restoration of our marriage. I wasn't suspicious, because his house was our home office, and we went back and forth during the day.

I had forgiven Jake and I wanted so much for our marriage to work out. After all, he was the love of my life and I couldn't bear living without him. God had done so much in my life that it was easy for me to accept his mistakes and to forgive him. I had taken responsibility for how my own behavior had contributed to the break in our marriage. I also felt that our marriage was worth saving, as we had been through a lot together with his health, raising a family and all the ups and downs of the business. This was just one more hurdle we needed to jump, in order to have a stronger marriage.

"FORGIVENESS IS THE KEY TO EMOTIONAL HEALING"

The separation was supposed to be for six months, but now it had been a year, and it was time for Jake to make a decision. We couldn't live continually in limbo; especially me, not knowing where I stood in my marriage. When we had a session with Jeanne on December 29, 2009, Jake was still unable to make up his mind. All this time, Jake never wanted to admit that he had done anything wrong. But on that day, Jake admitted that he had been wrong, and he asked me to forgive him, but he still couldn't say whether he wanted to be married or not. When I heard what he said, I not only cried for myself but also for our marriage, knowing that our marriage might be over. We scheduled another session in two weeks. Jeanne told Jake that he just couldn't prolong his decision any longer. It had been over a year, and that was enough time for him to think about what he wanted to do.

"YOU CAN'T FORCE LOVE; IT'S A VOLUNTARY ACT"

It had been a tradition for many years to host a New Year's Eve party in our home, so we could celebrate with our children and friends. I was hoping that Jake would make his mind up about our marriage tonight. He picked a fight with me instead, as an excuse to leave the house and go to a club with his friends. I swallowed my pride and begged him to stay, as I wanted to ring in the New Year with him. I couldn't talk him out of going, so he left to be with his friends. An hour later, Jake came home, as he felt he needed to celebrate New Year's Eve at home.

The next day, I noticed that Jake was wearing his wedding ring. Jake had taken his wedding ring off when he had neck surgery in July 2009, and he hadn't put it on again since then. When I saw the ring, I knew that he had made the commitment to stay in the marriage, and it was the happiest day of my life! I felt that we could start rebuilding our marriage now, and I was determined to make it work. Even the way that I was praying for my marriage had changed; I was now asking God to change me, so I could be a better person, wife and mother to my children. I wanted my family and marriage restored…I wanted my family back!

"LOVE = GIVE"

Two weeks later, at the counseling session, Jake told Jeanne about his intention to make the marriage work. It was a very good session. Towards the end of the session, Jeanne suggested that perhaps we should renew our vows. We both liked the idea and Jake wanted to do it right away. Because I didn't want to celebrate two anniversary dates, I wanted to wait until our anniversary in June. Jake agreed and we made plans to renew of our vows.

I was so happy that it just tickled my heart! I told a few friends that we were back together and we planned on renewing our vows. I started making plans for the party, such as who would do the ceremony, what food would be served and what dress I would like to wear. I thought of having it in our backyard at sunset with a little reception afterwards. I felt like I was on cloud nine and I dreamed about that day.

Even though Jake was home and he had made a commitment to stay in the marriage, I could still feel him holding back in the relationship. He would zone out watching TV and would just keep to himself. I knew that business was slow, so I gave him his space and justified his actions as being business related. I was happy just to have him and my family back together again.

While watching TV on the evening of April 27, 2010, Jake told me that he didn't feel right in his heart about renewing our vows. He didn't tell me why, even though we talked about it, but no conclusion was made.

"DON'T UNDERESTIMATE THE CALM WATERS, AS YOU DON'T KNOW HOW STRONG THE UNDERCURRENT IS"

I became very busy with preparations for a conference that I was hosting. It was attended by 500 people, so it was very successful. The last night of the conference, I was called up to the stage and everyone sang happy birthday to me. Jake gave me a very beautiful flower arrangement for my birthday, and that night we went out to dinner to celebrate. I had to get up early the next morning to take the speakers to the airport, and then I came home and slept.

Jake woke me up in the afternoon, so I could celebrate my birthday with my family. Jake gave me some gifts and so did my children. We all went out for dinner to celebrate, and it was the best birthday ever for me…I was in seventh heaven! Because everything seemed to be good now, I could continue planning my party.

"A BIRTHDAY IS A CELEBRATION OF LIFE, SO CELEBRATE YOU"

We didn't go to church on Mother's day, and the children cooked us breakfast. After breakfast, Jake went to the coffee shop to work and I went grocery shopping for dinner. Jake was gone all day, and when he came home around 5:30 PM, I was working in my office. He opened my office door and started yelling at me, and he told me that he couldn't stand me anymore. Jake accused me of trying to ruin the business for him. He said that I had made an employee quit, and he had to persuade that employee to stay.

Jake asked the kids if they wanted to go out for dinner with him, because he didn't want to see my face at all. I told Jake that I would go to church, and he could grill the steaks I had just gotten, because I figured it would calm him down. Jake packed that night and moved out of the house. I thought he was just angry and that he would come back. I guess I was wrong, because he never came back.

Jake told me that I had almost ruined his business this time, so I was not allowed to go back to the office. He hired a new office manager to replace me, and I was required to work at home, mostly doing the bookkeeping.

"YOU CAN'T CHANGE A PERSON, YOU ONLY CAN CHANGE YOU"

Our oldest son was graduating from high school that year and we were having a graduation party for him. Some of my friends suggested that I invite Jake's family, as it might make him happy, and perhaps it would be the very thing that would bring him back. I hadn't had any kind of relationship with his family for nine years, so this was a very hard thing for me to do. But I swallowed my pride, and I told Jake that he could invite his family to the graduation party. My friends and I prayed that God would give me grace when I saw them again.

I thank God that I am blessed with wonderful friends who are like family to me! On the day of the graduation party, my friends were at my house, giving me moral support. When the party was starting to dwindle down, I escaped to the bathroom to find some solitude. As I sat there resting, I took a deep breath…having Jake's family in my house that afternoon had been a big event. It was then that I heard the still small voice telling me that I was free. I had to think about what I had just heard, but then I heard it again…I was free. I knew God had set me free from my marriage that day; it was June 10, 2010.

Although I knew that I had clearly heard God telling me that I was free, I couldn't justify leaving the marriage based upon what I had heard that day. Deep in my heart, I was still hoping for the restoration of my marriage, so I wanted to make sure that I had peace before leaving.

"WHOMEVER HE SETS FREE IS FREE INDEED"

Once Jake left home, he had no contact with the kids for two months. At that time, he called a family meeting and explained to the kids that he loved them and what had happened between the two of us had nothing to do with them. Jake also felt a divorce would be better for all of us, because we didn't get along. Jake further said that there were 168 hours in the week and he only required 6 hours a week with the kids. On Wednesday nights, he would like to have dinner with them from 6 - 9 PM, and he wanted to take the kids to church on Sunday morning from 8:30 – 11:30 AM. It's interesting that he chose our former family night as one of his times to see the kids.

I still had a lot of my things at Jake's house, and I had to go there to pick up a few items for Joy's surprise birthday party. When

I went into the house, Jake asked me to sit down and have a talk with him. For thirty minutes, I listened to how the marriage break up was my fault; how he had come home and I hadn't changed; how he felt sorry for me, etc. Jake made it clear to me that he had moved on and that we would never get back together again.

I remember just sitting there listening to him. I didn't react, I was numb. I realized at that moment our marriage was over. I couldn't fall apart, as I had to go to Joy's house and get it ready for her surprise party. I thank God for friends who were willing to help me prepare for the party by cooking and decorating.

While we were waiting for the guests and Joy to arrive, I had a chance to lie down for twenty minutes. As soon as I lay down, I felt the harsh words that Jake had spoken rush over me. I was shaking inside and crying, but I had to conceal my tears, as no one knew what had happened that morning. Jake had a way of ruining the best days of my life with his words or actions.

"YOU DON'T ALWAYS HAVE CONTROL OVER WHAT HAPPENS TO YOU, BUT YOU CAN CHOOSE HOW YOU REACT TO IT"

A day after Joy's surprise birthday celebration, Mieke, who is like the little sister that I never had, moved to Boston with her family. I felt alone, because Mieke was always there to listen when I needed to unload my heart. It was difficult to see Mieke and her family leave, but I know that God was guiding them in this new chapter of their lives.

Our oldest son was going to college in Arizona, and we were planning a road trip to take him there. The children asked Jake if he would go with us, but he refused to go and, as usual, he used work as his excuse. The children were mad, but they couldn't say anything to him. So the children and I, plus my friend Mary, hit the road for a 10-day trip.

Even though I knew it was over, I still had faith that God could turn this around and save our marriage. I guess deep inside of my heart I wanted Jake to want me, because I thought I was worth it.

"NEVER STAY BECAUSE OF PITY; IT WON'T LAST"

Chapter 14

The Inevitable Divorce

We continued seeing Jeanne every two weeks, but we were back to square one again, since it was discovered that Jake had been involved in another affair. Jake was becoming more vocal about his intention of ending our marriage, and he told Jeanne that he didn't love me anymore. He just wanted out of the marriage, but he intended to take care of me and the children financially. He said that I would be able to live in the house, so the kids would have some stability.

Through our mutual friend and office manager, I found out Jake was having an affair with a twenty-four year old woman from Iran who he had been talking to since December 2009. Suddenly, I had flashbacks in my mind about all of the times that he couldn't make a decision to stay in our marriage. I now understood why he had distanced himself, even though he had come back. I remembered what the flower shop clerk had said to me about him picking up roses that I never received…and all the weekend disappearances to the health club.

"LOVE AND LUST CAN LOOK THE SAME, BUT ONE OF THEM IS A DESTROYER"

As the news about my divorce spread, more friends became aware of what was going on in my life. When I went out for lunch with my friend, Amy, she was nervous and made sure that I knew how much she loved and cared about me. I thought that was strange, but she finally told me how she had seen Jake kissing a girl in the health club parking lot a couple weeks ago. I didn't react to the news; in fact, I laughed and told her that I thought I had heard it all. God had really changed me and given me peace to go through this time.

After she had seen how Jake treated me, the office manager became my friend. One afternoon, when we had time to visit, she told me how beautiful I was and how I shouldn't take any more abuse from Jake. I had heard about abuse, but I didn't understand it completely. I always thought abuse was when someone hit you across the face. Jake never hit me, but he always criticized me about my weight, my voice, my laugh…even the way I sat. I never thought it was abuse until that day.

Something clicked in me and I suddenly realized that's what had happened to me during our marriage. I had been so naïve and oblivious to so many things. How could I not have seen it, when others saw it so clearly? I guess "love covers a multitude of sins" really was my blindfold. I never saw that Jake was doing anything wrong. In my eyes, he was a hard-working man who cared for and loved his family. He loved God and He knew what the Bible said, so I trusted that he wouldn't do anything outside of that context. Boy…was I wrong!

"GOD SEARCHES THE HEART AND TRIES THE MIND"

I can't change another person, but I certainly had the power to change me. I was responsible for who I was and how I wanted to be treated. For all these years, I had allowed Jake to treat me poorly, because I didn't know any better. I was a naïve, young woman who knew nothing about America, and I couldn't see the world beyond the four walls of my home, which was also my workplace. When I heard the talk about Jake, I always thought people were just jealous of his success. In my eyes, Jake had always been my prince charming and he couldn't do anything wrong.

I continued to pray and stand in faith, believing God that Jake would come back. When I felt the nudge in my heart one day, I called Jake, he picked up the phone and we talked. Jake assured me that there was nothing left between us and that he had moved on. He said that he didn't love me, but he cared about me, and if I gave him a divorce, he would take care of me and the children financially. I accepted his offer and told him that I wouldn't contest the divorce. I advised Jake to search his heart to be certain that he was supposed to be with this woman. He told me that when he had prayed about it, God had told him that she was the right one for him and that marrying me had been the mistake. I told Jake to mark the date of this conversation down, because he could refer back to it in a few years and he would find the truth.

I didn't think our marriage had been a mistake; what we had done in our marriage was the mistake. We neglected our relationship and took each other for granted. I believe that God had put us together, because He had plans for us and for our children. Without our union, the children wouldn't have been born, but God saw and knew our children before time began. Even if our marriage had been a mistake, God had caused everything to work out for good; we have four beautiful children and a successful business and ministry.

I had come to accept the fact that divorce was inevitable. Jake assured me that we could remain friends, there would be a fair division of assets and he would take care of me. During the conversation, he also mentioned that he had seen a lawyer and he would be serving me divorce papers. Jake asked me if I wanted him to hand the paper to me or if I would prefer a courier. I told him to serve me the papers the proper way.

I really didn't know what to think or how to feel…I was numb and emotionally and physically tired from the first affair. I didn't have it in me to fight for my marriage a second time around. I came to peace with the fact that I would be divorced and raising my children alone, which is what I had done all along. Jake hadn't been there for us in a long time, so there wouldn't be much difference. I could beg him to stay or try to make a deal with him, but in the end, he would eventually leave anyhow. If he was that miserable and unhappy with me, why hold him back? With some hope that this could still turn around, I decided to let him go.

"YOU HAVE TO LET GO, TO FIND OUT WHAT TRULY BELONGS TO YOU"

Two months after that conversation, Jake served me with divorce papers. Even though I had prepared myself for the divorce, I still wasn't ready. When I was handed the divorce papers, I was in shock. I called Joy and her words calmed me, like they always have. Then I called Jan, who helped me find my first attorney, and she accompanied me to the first meeting. The attorney asked me to write my life story down for the deposition. I didn't know why I should do that, after all, the deposition was for a divorce. I wasn't really up for the divorce. There was a lot of paperwork to go through, lots of copies to be made and questions that had to be answered. I felt like I was the one on the witness stand, and I was humiliated by having to answer all of those questions. I felt like I was a criminal on trial, having to always defend myself.

During this difficult time, a friend of mine, Tammy, mentioned that she knew a counselor who had a track record for saving marriages, and she asked me if I would be willing to talk with him. I told her that I would try anything that might save my marriage, and I hoped this counselor would be the one who could help pull my marriage back together. The problem now was convincing Jake to go back to counseling again. To my surprise, Jake agreed to go with me for three sessions, but only if the counselor could prescribe medication.

In our first session, Jake made sure that the counselor understood that he didn't want reconciliation. His only reason for being there was to request that the counselor prescribe medication for me. I knew I didn't need any medication, but I was willing to take it to save my marriage. The counselor looked at Jake and said he wasn't going to do that. Jake only went to counseling for the three sessions that he had agreed to, but I continued to see the counselor, as I needed it for my sanity…I needed someone who I could talk to.

Chapter 15

Free at Last

Well, our divorce process didn't go quite as anticipated. All the promises Jake had made to the counselors were only spoken words. As the divorce progressed and the days passed, the process got uglier and uglier. I had to make tons of copies of requested documents and some of them they already had. There were accusations made about me stealing the company's money, and I had to prove myself by showing every piece of evidence that Jake requested. This was the man that told me he trusted me with his money. I was angry at him for putting me in this situation, but I had to do what the attorney requested. I thought it was going to be easy; we would divide the assets and go our separate ways. After all, I was giving him what he wanted…a divorce.

"AN ACTION CAN REVEAL WHAT'S TRULY IN THE HEART"

I wondered who this was that I was dealing with, because this wasn't the same man I had married. I came to realize that a promise didn't mean anything to Jake. He would say things he wanted me to hear and agreed to what he wanted me to do, but any proposal from Jake wasn't fair. At this time, I soon realized that I needed a new attorney to deal with Jake. As usual, Joy came to my rescue, when she referred me to the attorney who helped me finish my divorce.

I stayed home during the divorce, and I was glad that I had, because I could help my children through the fallout. The impact of the divorce was very hard on the children, as they were confused and angry and felt the divorce was their fault. I had been on an emotional roller coaster for years myself, but now the children had joined me on this wild ride. When I cried, I didn't cry just for myself...it was for my children too. No matter what people say, the impact of divorce is hard on everyone involved, leaving scarred hearts in its wake and shattering trust like glass, which is nearly impossible to repair.

"THINGS YOU CRY ABOUT NOW, MAY ACTUALLY BE THE THINGS YOU'RE GRATEFUL FOR LATER"

I held onto God as tightly as I could during all of this, because I knew He was the only one who could carry me through this ordeal. At night, He always granted me a deep, restful sleep; in the morning, He would give me the grace I needed for that day. I could see His hand upon me, which made it easier for me to walk through this, and I knew He would be there for me all the way to the end.

Going through the dark tunnel of divorce, wasn't easy for me, especially when there was no light at the end of the tunnel. It was very painful, but during this process, I had to allow God to work on my wounded heart and deal with my emotional overload. There were times when I wished that this horrific nightmare would just go away, but no matter how hard I wished, I still had to deal with the gruesome divorce process.

"THE DARKEST TIME IS WHEN YOU GO THROUGH THE TUNNEL OF TRIALS"

Yet, deep down in my heart, I still wished that Jake would change his mind about reconciling. I guess I knew it would never happen though, as he was determined to get a divorce. I had to go through court and mediation for the divorce process. Through all of this, I was incredibly blessed to have friends who would pray for me, comfort me and be there for me when I needed them. At times, I was very fearful about what would happen when I had a court appearance, but God would assure me that everything would be okay, and I could see how He had turned things around for me. The results sometimes weren't what I had anticipated, but when I looked back, I could see His hand guiding me.

The divorce proceedings went on for two years. Jake had four attorneys representing him during that time, and each time he hired a new attorney, it required time for them to study the case. After a while, the time and money spent on the court appearances and mediations were draining me mentally, physically and emotionally... I was getting tired of it all.

The divorce paper was drafted three times and I signed it each time. Jake would then change his mind about issues that we had agreed upon, so we would have to go to back to the negotiation table again. Even though Jake wanted the divorce, I realized that he just couldn't cut the ties.

Divorce is a funny thing…people want to get divorced because they think it's the answer to all of their problems. Yet when faced with the reality and finality of divorce, they freeze and can't do it, knowing that it's the end of a relationship that was once their hope for a future. There's no winner in a divorce; both parties are casualties when the relationship fails. I realized what was going on with Jake, and I was getting tired of being dragged down the muddy path of divorce. I wished that it would all just end, because I just couldn't go through the mediation process again.

So I talked with my attorney and I told him that this divorce needed to be over. I wanted to get off the roller coaster ride I had been on, and I wanted to move on with my life. I had asked God to clean me up, heal me and change me, while I was going through the tunnel of divorce, so that when I came out, I would be able to live my life, chase my dreams and fulfill my destiny in Him.

"THERE IS LIGHT AT THE END OF THE TUNNEL ~ KEEP GOING"

Once again, the divorce paper was drafted with some changes that we had made. I had signed it, but Jake hadn't. My attorney and I agreed that we needed to give to Jake a timeline in which to sign the divorce papers, and in doing so, we petitioned the court to order Jake to sign the papers. During this entire grueling process, I still had a flicker of hope in the corner of my heart that Jake would change his mind, but that was soon extinguished.

Two days before the court date on April 5, 2012, Jake signed the divorce papers. A big sigh…I was free at last! It was a bittersweet feeling, as I was a free woman now, yet I cried for the demise of my marriage. The divorce had caused some of the darkest hours of my life; it was like a repeating nightmare, haunting me night after night…and now it had finally ended.

Yes…I am finally free! I feel like a bird that has just been released from its cage. There is a new perspective and horizon from the tops of the trees, and I realized that there is a whole new world out there for me to explore…and I am ready!

"THE END DOESN'T NEED TO BE FEARED; IT'S JUST THE BEGINNING OF SOMETHING NEW"

Chapter 16

I Found the Fortune

N ow that I'm a free woman, I contemplate what I would like to do next. I am feeling somewhat lost, as I don't really have a decisive career path. I have lived in the shadow of someone who I thought the world of, but with that covering removed now, I feel naked and frozen in the moment of my freedom.

I felt like someone had opened the door to my jail cell and told me to go free. I know that I'm free to walk or run out, yet I am standing there, frozen in unbelief. I am finally free, but I'm also afraid to step out of my prison and face the unknown. The jail is familiar to me, because that's all I've known, and I am comfortable with it. Although I know there is a better life and many opportunities out there for me, fear of the unknown still grips me.

With fear and anticipation, and yet with excitement for everything that's out there, I gather myself up and take the first step of faith out of the door. I made the decision that it was time for me to move on, so I searched the horizon and focused on the promise of the rainbow that there's something even better out there for me, as I dared to move toward my dreams and destiny.

"AFTER EVERY STORM, THERE'S A RAINBOW OF PROMISE"

I thought it would be easy to just get out and take on the world. I was free to do what I wanted to now, but I found out it was easier to say than do. I feel stuck now, and I don't know which direction to turn. A few of my friends encouraged me to do real estate again, but I know in my heart that it's not my passion anymore…that season is over.

I used to enjoy real estate with all its excitement; it was never boring. Each file had a character all of its own, because not all buyers or sellers were the same. It wasn't a cookie-cutter business, because you are dealing with real people with real issues. I enjoyed taking buyers through houses and seeing the excitement in their eyes when they discovered their dream home. I also sensed the sigh of relief from the sellers at closing, knowing that they could move on with their lives in a new home, new area, etc.

I tried to pick myself up by continuing my education, so I could do real estate again. Even though I knew my heart wasn't fully in it, I did what I needed to do to earn income to take care of my family. I thought this would be easy, so I joined the best real estate team in town and I was ready to go. The reality was that it was difficult to work in real estate when my heart wasn't in it.

"WHERE THERE'S NO PASSION, NOTHING GROWS"

In my case, divorce was a blessing from God. No, it doesn't mean that I endorse divorce, as I'm a firm believer that marriage is an "until death do us part" commitment. But things happen in our lives that we can't avoid, and we can't possibly control another person's decisions. I have learned that it's not marriage or the vows that change…it's the people that change. All I can do is pick up the pieces of my broken heart and nurture my emotional pain, giving it all to God. He is the Master Potter, and He makes all things beautiful and new again in their time. Even though the scars remain, the painful sting is gone.

"GOD MADE A BEAUTIFUL TAPESTRY FROM TORN PIECES"

As I looked back on the last 27 years of my life, and how I was uprooted and planted in America, I see God's hand upon my life. He provided friends to help me through many lonely days and people who have helped me grow in my walk with God. I have been healed and released from the anger, fear, rejection, and bitterness that the divorce had caused.

It's funny how we all have preconceived ideas and plans about what our lives should be, would be, might be and could be, but life is always full of unexpected surprises. I stand amazed at all of the things that I'm doing now, which I hadn't previously thought about or even imagined doing. The day He made me, God determined what gifts and talents He would bestow upon me, yet those gifts and talents have remained buried until due time.

I never thought in a million years that writing would be something that I enjoyed doing. In school, writing was something that I dreaded, because I wasn't very good at it. In fact, I couldn't even write a two-page story, let alone a book. But God has mysterious ways of doing things, and He tricked me into writing a journal since 2008. While I was going through my separation, I had to write things down, so I could remember what I had prayed for and the word that He had given me for that day.

"GIFTS AND TALENTS ARE BURIED UNTIL DUE TIME"

My first attorney asked me to write my life story for the deposition, which became the outline for this book. I started to write comments on a blog that I followed, and I realized that I had followers after a while, who enjoyed reading what I had to say. My writing seems to naturally flow, as I find it easy to convey my thoughts and feelings about a subject.

Life has been good to me and I am happier now that I am free. I still have my struggles, but life has more meaning and purpose, since I found my passion for writing. What I have experienced in my life may help others see the light at the end of their dark tunnels. I pray that it will give them the hope they need to dream again, so they can also pursue their unique destinies. Only by the grace of God, and my willingness to bear it all with Him, has this diamond in the rough been polished and come out shining brilliantly for His glory.

"LIFE IS ART AND FULL OF COLOR"

I am excited as I embark upon a new journey on uncharted waters. I feel like a butterfly, emerging from its cocoon, strengthening its wings as fluid pumps into them, so it can fly and explore the world out there. I still don't know what the next chapter of my life will bring, but I do know that I have a purpose and destiny to fulfill.

"WHEN YOU LET GO OF WHAT'S IN YOUR HANDS, GOD RELEASES WHAT'S IN HIS HANDS"

Throughout all of this, I have found the fortune or myself…the one who is fearfully and wonderfully made. The utmost fortune is found when you discover who you are inside out. I've had quite an extraordinarily colorful life full of twists and turns, ups and downs, mountain highs and valley lows. Would I trade it for anything else? Nah…I love my life! ☺

"A LIFETIME OF HAPPINESS LIES AHEAD OF YOU"

About Susy

Susy Pujiro is the mother of four beautiful children and owner of four dogs that are loved very much. Susy worked in the real estate business for 22 years, but after the divorce, she found and is pursuing the passion of her heart in writing. This book is about Susy's life, her struggles through the divorce, and how she emerged from that pit as a polished diamond, shining brightly for God's glory.

To contact Susy Pujiro:

Email: susysblog@gmail.com
Follow her blog: susysthinkingplace.com
Twitter: @susypujiro